MORIAH J. HAGEL

To Live

FINDING THE MIND OF CHRIST

IRON STREAM

Birmingham, Alabama

To Live: Finding the Mind of Christ

Iron Stream
An imprint of Iron Stream Media
100 Missionary Ridge
Birmingham, AL 35242
IronStreamMedia.com

Iron Stream Media serves its authors as they express their views, which may not express the views of the publisher.

Library of Congress Control Number: 2026931994

Cover design by www.BookCoverDesign.us

ISBN: 978-1-56309-802-4 (paperback)
ISBN: 978-1-56309-803-1 (eBook)

1 2 3 4 5—30 29 28 27 26

"This inspiring little volume tackles the big questions head-on: *What are you living for? Where is your identity found? Whom do you love more than God?* And so much more. In forty-two lessons from the book of Philippians, author Moriah Hagel shares openly and honestly from her own experiences and from her years of study in God's Word. As you read, you'll be encouraged, you'll be challenged, and you'll undoubtedly be changed for good in all the ways that matter for eternity."

—Ann Tatlock, novelist, children's author, editor, writing mentor

"'They leave a good name for God wherever they go.' As I think about Hagel's passionate challenge for us all 'to live' and to pursue the mind of Christ, this compelling, yet beautiful quote from her work describing those who do is forever etched in my mind. Moriah shares genuine personal reflection with each day of this forty-two-day study for young women, and the focus of each day is truly worth a year of deep personal reflection. I am grateful for this daily guide to live as Christ and believe other readers of this work will also be called to live!"

—Jean-Noel Thompson, PhD, executive vice president at Harding University

"Moriah Hagel has 'reached for the stars' once again. Her thought-provoking yet pragmatic devotional book leads the reader toward enjoying forty-two days of finding the mind of Christ. A must-read for anyone desiring a more holy life."

—Dr. Neal Hughes, DMin, director of missions, Montgomery Baptist Association

"In *To Live*, Moriah Hagel once again challenges the reader to look inward and reconsider what it means to live in Christ. Its daily readings are deeply rooted in the Word of God; yet they are intimate and personal, reflecting the author's own walk of faith. The premise of the book is a deeper examination of the apostle Paul's statement, 'For to me to live is Christ, and to die is gain' (Philippians 1:21 ESV). Readers will be encouraged, inspired, and challenged by this book."

—Doug Chappelle, pastor, Thelma Baptist Church

Lord, this book is for You and to You. Please use it for Your glory to touch and change lives for your Kingdom. May all who read it grow closer to the mind of Your Son, Jesus Christ.

Philippians 1:21: "For to me, to live is Christ, and to die is gain."

What are we truly living for?

Contents

Foreword

I cannot remember the precise time I first took notice of the scriptural challenge from the apostle Paul to "let this mind be in you which was also in Christ Jesus" (Philippians 2:5), but I am confident it has been more than four decades. (Yes, I really am an old codger now.) Like Jesus's mother, Mary, I have pondered it in my heart ever since, wondering just what it could mean. I initially supposed it to mean to think like Jesus thought, which posed yet another series of questions in my mind, such as, *How is that even possible, since Jesus is God in human flesh and I am a mere mortal with a very finite brain?* However, after a more careful reading of the context of this challenge, it seems more likely to me now that Paul is calling Christians to exemplify humility and subjection to the will of God, the Father, just as Jesus did and continues to do even now from His seat at the Father's right hand.

Consider the enormity of this mindset: even though Jesus was and is God in human flesh, He demonstrated humility in a multitude of ways during His earthly life, from His extremely humble birth in a stable with a manger for a crib to His washing of His disciples' nasty feet at the Last Supper to His willing submission to the ultimate enemy of all: death on the cross at the hands of sinful men. To have the mind of Christ, then, we must imitate Jesus's humility as much as His righteousness, which does not mean making ourselves a doormat for anyone who comes along but rather to know and understand our rightful place in God's plan for the world and for us as individuals living within it.

I do not pretend to have a full grasp of how to live out this example of Jesus, even after a lifetime of contemplating and attempting it, but my understanding has slowly evolved to its present position of believing it means to strive to imitate Jesus's thinking and example of humble submission to God's will as much as we can. Jesus demonstrated a balance of both mercy and justice to all He met. He showed gentleness and mercy to the humble and penitent, and He showed stern justice to the proud, self-righteous, and impenitent. Jesus lived out supreme righteousness with humility and commanded all who followed Him as disciples—which now includes you and me—to live righteously and humbly as well. It is quite a challenge indeed!

After meeting Moriah Hagel at the Blue Lake Christian Writers Conference in March 2025, and subscribing to her family blog for Christian living, I have come to admire and respect her and her entire family as excellent examples of Christlikeness who demonstrate the mind of Christ in their daily Christian lives. Moriah's breadth of Bible knowledge and depth of spiritual maturity is especially evidenced by her application of the Scriptures in her writings, not only on her blog but within the pages of this current Bible study that you are about to begin. I really cannot express well enough how impressed I am with Moriah's competent ability to "rightly [divide] the word of truth" (2 Timothy 2:15), and I think you will be, too, as you progress through this in-depth study of Paul's epistle to the church in Philippi and, ultimately, to each of us today. As a result of completing this Bible study, I pray that, like Moriah, you and I will be better examples of Christlikeness as we endeavor to practice having the mind of Christ in our daily Christian living.

Michael L. White
Your Humble Aspirer

Preface

Dear fellow Christians,

To Live began in a Bible study when my sister asked a simple question about Paul's confounding statement: "To live is Christ, and to die is gain" (Philippians 1:21). She asked us what we were living for. Was it relationships, sports, school, family, our jobs, careers, or Christ and only Christ? I had to look inside a spiritual mirror and examine my life. What was I living for? I found that whatever I was living for is where I found my identity. Have you ever introspectively looked at yourself? I would encourage you to do so, because if we find our "to live" is in anything but Christ, then when we die, it will not be gain for us, it will be hell. This mindset is a little hard to wrap my head around sometimes because what I am living for are good things, but I know I need and want to have the mind of Christ, so that I, too, like Paul, can say, "To live is Christ, and to die is gain." This is not to argue with how salvation is obtained or any of that; this book is simply to help us as we live here on this earth to have our minds and identity transformed into the mind of Christ.

This book is one geared to help each of us gain the mind of our Savior in our pursuit of Christ. This mindset will anchor our identity to Christ as we explore how He thought and responded. So often we are overwhelmed by what the world or others say we are or are not to be, but God has set us free. He has designed us for a purpose beyond ourselves. Yet to discover that purpose, we must discover who He calls us to be, what our true identity is. He is the designer of our identity, and we can only find who we are truly meant to be when we find ourselves in Him. Obtaining the mind of Christ is not something we can gain simply by determination and cognitive choices. Rather it is something that can only be obtained through the permission and power of Jesus Christ. He is the One who will teach us how to have His mindset. As we walk through the applications, I would encourage each of you to do this prayerfully so that change can take place in both your hearts and minds as we seek the mind of Christ. When we seek Him diligently, He will have mercy on us and give us our petition. "Seek first the kingdom of God and His righteousness, and all these things will be added to you" (Matthew 6:33). I hope you are as challenged as I was and that you choose to hang in there with God through thick and thin as He refines your thinking and your mindset.

May God find our minds ready to be guided by Him and in a place ready for His work. May He prepare your hearts as you walk through this process and give you the endurance needed as you reach for the goal of finding your identity in Christ through obtaining His mindset. May He encourage you on this journey and allow you to see the work that He will do in you as you press into Him and never stop striving to have the mind of Christ. May God grant you the endurance and strength to run well.

Acknowledgments

Thank you to Sethany Perdue for teaching the Bible study on Philippians and sharing what God had on your heart that day. To Julie Hagel and Charisa Hagel for your insights, help, and editing of the first draft. To all those who allowed me to use your stories to bless others so that we all may learn from the examples you set and grow in obtaining the mind of Christ. Thank you.

Day One

An Encouragement

Philippians 1:3

I thank my God upon every remembrance of you.

There is one military family I know from Hawaii about whom, every time I think about them, I have nothing but good things to say, and my heart rejoices over what God has done and is doing through them. They were the military chaplain family who served at the base we were at for two or three years. They bubble over with the joy of the Lord and with humility. Serving God at whatever base they are stationed at, they leave a good name for God wherever they go. This chaplain could tell you that you were headed for hell without Jesus, and you loved him for it because somehow you could feel the hope that he was offering through Jesus. But even amazing servants of God have hard days and need prayers. Just because we are following Jesus does not mean our lives will be easy. In fact, scripture tells us, as Christians, our lives will have challenges, hard ones (John 16:33). Therefore, we should continue to lift up our brothers and sisters in Christ even when it seems like they have "got it." Because not everyone who seems like they have it together really does. We are all struggling in one way or another, but how we endure the struggle and where we choose to place our identity will help determine how it all comes out. When I became a young adult, I found myself getting agitated about my world changing. Not only were things not as simple anymore, but they were also overwhelming. I began feeling misplaced. New people came into my world and appeared to be absorbing everything. I did not feel like I had a place anymore. I felt overlooked and left out of my own world as if I were a stranger in it. But God taught me not to dwell on what others might think about me. Ephesians 6:6 encourages us not to act as men pleasers: doing things because of something we imagine. Instead, we are to act in a manner that honors God, and we are to do it with a willing heart. I did not need to be concerned if they overlooked me on purpose, but I was to jump in and be the encouragement for them, to do to others what you would have them do to you, as the Golden Rule says. My identity could not be found in others' opinions of me or how well I was liked or disliked. It had to be found in the truth that I was a child of God. God called me to get out of my feelings and get busy serving Him by serving His people.

Paul, the author of the book of Philippians, while in jail, wrote to the believers to encourage them. He could have focused on so many things, yet he took time to thank God for the believers in Philippi. We can learn from Paul's example to give thanks in everything (Philippians 4:6). When I was a child, my mom used to make me say three things nice about something every time I complained about it. This practice was to teach me gratitude, which is something Paul is demonstrating even while in prison. He was counting his blessings to keep his mind in a position of gratitude to the Father. The focus of gratitude is essential to finding our identity in Christ. In life, as we walk through difficulties, we will get the opportunity to discover whom God has designed us to be by trusting Him through the pain and the struggle, looking for the goodness of God, and saying thank You. This is one key step to finding the mind of Christ. Also, no matter our circumstances, we can always be praying for others. This helps not only the ones we pray for but also us; a Holy Spirit spark begins to burn and it takes our focus off our situation and puts it on to the bigger picture. Before the trial and crucifixion, John records that while Jesus was praying for the cup of suffering to be taken away, He spent an entire chapter praying for us (John 17). Christ spent the last moments before He was beaten and crucified praying for us. We ought to do the same. In the middle of hardship, we should pray for others. This life is not about us. It is about God.

According to 1 Peter 2:9 we are "a chosen generation, a royal priesthood, a holy nation, His own special people, that [we] may proclaim the praises of Him who called [us] out of darkness into His marvelous light." As representatives of Christ (the priests), we are to live as Christ did and to be an example to others. How do we do that? We pray to have the mind of Christ. James 1:5 tells us that we simply need to ask for God's wisdom because He gives liberally to those who are asking. But let us not just ask for wisdom; let us apply it to our lives. We know from scripture that Jesus prayed for others, healed others, and served others. He went to great lengths to be an example for us. He told and showed us the greatest commandment, which is to love God with all our heart, mind, and soul. And the second is like it, to love our neighbor as ourselves (Matthew 22:37–39). That is how we need to live: God first and others second. We must make sure to keep these in their proper order. It is vital that we not rank people above Jesus in our lives because we do not live for them. We live for God. People cannot define us. God created us, and He defines our identity. He calls it out from deep within us through His Word, His love, trials, hardships, relationships, events of life, and so on. The trials, hardships, relationships, and events do not create our identity, but rather God uses them to show us His identity for us, if we will trust Him through it. It is the Lord who will be able to fashion and form us into what He intends for us to be.

Because we are to love Him first, we first give thanks to Him and then make our request known to heaven for ourselves and others (Philippians 4:6). Placing God first keeps our mind in the attitude of Christ's. Constant praise and thanksgiving are excellent ways for changing our perspective on what is going on in our lives. Find something to praise. Look around; there is always something, even if it is simply that we are breathing. Praise God because of flowers, because of sunsets or sunrises, because of the beauty of the oceans or the majesties of the mountains and cliffs. One way I choose to keep my mindset in one of praise is to keep a gratitude journal. Write things down as you think of them or when you start or end your day. If you write down three things a day, you will have a thousand things within one year. Another attribute we can praise Him for is that He knows best (Jeremiah 29:11). My last summer in college, I worked a job and, on my lunch break, would run into the same kid. As I usually did, I would ask him how he was doing. The very first time he said, "all right." My response was, "Just all right?" Then I told him that he was breathing, which meant he was "blessed." After that it was on, you could see it on his face. Every day when I would ask how he was doing, he would find something else to say other than "blessed." But even though he did not say it, it did not stop the truth: that we all are blessed for the opportunity to live and serve God another day. If we are breathing, then we are blessed because God has chosen to give us another day to live for Him. And when you get tired, remember: our strength comes from the LORD, and we can praise Him for that too (Psalm 46:1).

Application: If Christ takes the time to pray for us before facing the cross, can't we take time in our struggles to pray for others? It will help us get our mind off ourselves and put it where it is supposed to be: on God and the needs of others. As a "royal priesthood," one of our jobs is to make intercession on behalf of others (1 Timothy 2:1). Ask a friend how you can be praying for them. As you hear prayer requests, you will find that there are more needed prayers than you will have time for, so start praying! Also put into practice praying your thanks to God. When was the last time you stopped in your prayer of wants and needs to just give Him thanks or praise for who He is and what He does? Let's make it happen! Think about these questions and write down your answers.

How does encouraging someone and praying for someone define your identity in Christ?

Who is one person whom you can be praying for and making intersession for?

What do they need prayer about?

Day Two

Submitting to a Faithful God

Philippians 1:6

Being confident of this very thing, that He who has begun a good work in you will complete it until the day of Jesus Christ.

I love this verse because it gives me hope. Despite my failings, God will complete what He has started as long as I continue to pursue Him and His desires (Proverbs 24:16). Remember how we said we could be thankful for another day to serve Him? I am especially thankful for those when I fail. When I would mess up as a child—like being rude to someone, because I did not always think before I spoke—my Mom would correct me and always give me another chance to do something good to "make it right," to say something nice. God's work in us is never incomplete. He always finishes the job and always gives us opportunities to do well today.

Recently, God asked me to give up a romantic relationship for Him and His plan for me. Through this, God wanted to do a growing work in me, but I had to obey for the work to be complete. It was painful. This was a long process, and I had many failings, tests, and struggles with who I was, who I wanted to be, and who God was calling me to be. I struggled, but God stayed with me, literally. Every time something happened, and I would take it to Him crying, He would quietly listen and then somehow give me the strength I needed to continue walking in obedience.

God is faithful. I love those words, "God is faithful." He used my anxieties and my failures to propel me toward Him and teach me that I was to be His. I was not this man's girlfriend first, but I was God's first. If I had let anything come first, before God in my life, then my feet would not be set on God and my identity would be built on shaky ground. I would be like that foolish man in the Bible who built his house on the shifting sand and not on the Rock (Matthew 7:24–27). Without His firm foundation, under the pressure that I did and would go through, I would have given way. It was hard enough to stay grounded with Christ, but He was faithful to complete His good work in me when I chose to be submitted to His will, His hand, and His way instead of my own. I had to take the first step of obedience and then lean on His strength to continually climb this spiritual mountain ahead of me. Through many tears and months of staying surrendered, God brought me through. He got me up the mountain; I just had to keep climbing with Him.

Isaiah talks about God telling the people of Israel that, when hardship comes, He will deliver (Isaiah 60:22). His hand is not shortened (Isaiah 59:1); He always accomplishes what He has said He will do. God said He would deliver the people of Israel out of Egypt, and He did (Exodus 3). Since He is faithful to accomplish what He starts, why do we find it so hard to trust Him? Because we are not rooted in Him, living in Him 100 percent of the way.

Who are we surrendering our lives and our will to? I believe we find it so hard to live for Christ and to trust Him because we still struggle with living for ourselves over God. We think we know best, but in reality, His plans are always best. Our flesh wars against the soul (Galatians 5:17); it does not want to submit to the will of God, but we must rule over the flesh. Scripture tells us that those who are Christ's crucify the flesh and its desires (Galatians 5:24). We are reminded in James to submit to God and draw near to Him, and when we do that He will draw near to us (James 4:7–8). That ought to be incentive enough, but that *submit* thing is difficult because it is a surrendering of our will to God. That should make it OK, but submitting to someone else who is not us can be very difficult to do. It is giving up control. It is doing not what we want but the will of the Father. Jesus, our example, in the garden of Gethsemane, gave up His will and said, "Your will be done" (Luke 22:42). This is not an easy task but one God asks each of us to do. My walking away from the relationship I was in when God asked me to was an act of submission to Him. I broke my own heart, but submission to God and His will is paramount in training ourselves to have the mind of Christ and becoming the women God wants us to be.

Sometimes this training comes through submitting to people God has placed as our spiritual leaders. However, when God is leading through people who are flawed, which He usually does, we have a very difficult time giving up our will for theirs. Remember, we must always keep God first. If we have Christ's mind within us, we are not giving up our will for someone else; we are giving up our will for Him. We are not surrendering to them but to God. Double check to know what God's will is, but when we know, we submit to the will of God for us because He is eternal love, goodness, and faithfulness. He knows tomorrow, what is best, and what will prepare us for His glory and His future plans for our lives.

Application: Isaiah 35:8 says that even a fool will not go astray on the highway of holiness. Trust that God will complete His masterpiece in you. Thank Him for it. Now pray for a humble and submissive heart to be moldable. Ask Him to continue to mold and shape you into His likeness. You can help this by deciding that in the next hardship you walk through, or perhaps one you are walking through now, you will choose to ask God what He wants you to learn from it instead of trying to get out of it.

How does being a Christian submitted to God shape your identity?

Where is one area that you need practice in being humble?

What are two ways you are going to work on that area to be more humble like Christ?

Day Three

Speaking in Love

Philippians 1:9–10

And this I pray, that your love may abound still more and more in knowledge and all discernment, that you may approve the things that are excellent, that you may be sincere and without offense till the day of Christ.

The year after I published my first book, I was given a great opportunity to teach a ladies' Sunday school class for the summer. This was an honor, not only to teach a class but also because most of the ladies were at least fifteen to twenty years older than I was and they allowed me to teach them. They were to let, in essence, a young Timothy come and teach. And like Timothy, I wondered how a young woman could be able to teach these women. The study we did had many difficult topics, especially for a single young woman. How was I to teach mature women, who had adult experiences different from my life experiences? So I asked God to help me teach them. After previously spending two years in class together, I had learned to love them. God used this love to better my teaching. I did not want to hurt them with the convicting message God had given me to teach, but when the Lord has spoken, who can but speak it (Amos 3:8)? Praise God, He gave me parables, stories, and acronyms to teach the hard truth in love and grace to the humble ladies who would submit themselves to be led by someone potentially half their age.

Love lightens the blow but still delivers it for the betterment of the one who is loved. While I want to be seen as the best example of this love, I am somewhere in the middle. Sometimes I wish I was more gentle in my response, and sometimes I want to be more resolute, but God asks us to put aside how we want to respond or be seen and to respond as Jesus did: in love. God is love (1 John 4:16). Paul prays that the Christians abound and live in the love of God. Because in His perfect love there is no guile, He discerns that which is excellent and knows how to be sincere. My sister described it as a love with no blinders. He sees us for who we are and knows our imperfections, yet still He loves us. With this accepting love we can speak to other Christians in love to point out the areas that they need to work on, not to cause an offense but because we love them and want to see them grow in Christ. Paul corrected Peter when the fisherman behaved contrary to what his own preaching was (Galatians 2:11–14). Paul called Peter out because in that moment Peter forgot who his identity was in. They had been teaching Christ, but when Jewish brothers came, Peter behaved as one who found his worth in his Jewish heritage, above his life in Christ. We can do this so often in our own lives as we find our identity in our religion, our livelihood, our friends, and more. Paul had to remind Peter where his identity was found and to live it out for new believers to see. With their examples, new Christians could learn that their identity does not come from others or even the standards of others, but from God and His values. They would not become slaves in bondage to the law of the Jewish people. Christ did not ask them to do that; He asked them (and us) to walk in freedom with Him to become who He wanted them to be.

Through the love of Christ we are to discern between what is good and right without condemnation. As we know what is right and wrong, and choose to walk in what is right, we will have joy and peace. We can be confident in the truth God has given us and remember to deliver it with love and grace. First

Corinthians 16:14 reminds us to let all that we do be done in love. This knowledge and discerning love teaches us how to speak the truth in love. As we love our brothers and sisters, we want to see them grow in Christ; but we don't want to crush their tender faith, so we learn to speak in such a way that will cause the least offense so that they may hear the truth. How do we make it palatable without depriving it of the nutrients? We choose to be in step with God, just as Christ was. In John 16:13, Jesus speaks of sending the Holy Spirit, the Spirit of truth, who "will guide you into all truth." Through Christ and the Holy Spirit we can discern and through Scripture we can know what is acceptable, but to have this balance of understanding we must first have a relationship with Christ. As we get to know Him, we will learn what He considers excellent. Like David asked in the Psalms, teach me Your ways, O God, and help me walk in Your precepts (Psalm 25:4–5).

When we see things through God's eyes we can be confident in who He has made us to be. That in turn allows us to live in His light and serve others better. One day at my receptionist job, a client was very mad at me. Instead of correcting the individual in the small areas where they were wrong, God gave me ears to actually hear what was really going on. When I understood why the individual was so angry, I could show compassion, and we ended the conversation amicably, actually praying on the phone over the real issue. When we see things through the light of God's eyes, it takes us out of the picture, and puts Christ at the center of it. John 6:63 says, "It is the Spirit who gives life; the flesh profits nothing." We are to stay focused on Him. We no longer see with just physical eyes but with spiritual eyes too. The book of Romans tells us that "those who live according to the flesh set their minds on the things of the flesh, but those who live according to the Spirit, the things of the Spirit" (Romans 8:5).

Application: Pray for God to show you where you need His love in knowledge and discernment. David prayed, "Examine me, O LORD, and prove me" (Psalm 26:2). Also pray for the holy balance of truth and love so that when we speak into others' lives, they get the perfect dosage of sincerity without offense. This is really important: make sure to stop when the Holy Spirit says to stop. If we don't, they will not get the right combination of truth and love. Once I was trying to encourage my friend. I gave her love and truth but kept talking for several minutes. When I finally stopped, our topic focus had changed from God to something else entirely. I had messed up and did not stop when the Holy Spirit prompted me to, which minimized the truth He wanted me to tell her. When we know who we are in Christ, and when we are searching for our identity by thinking about the thoughts and the mind of Christ, we will be able to obey the Holy Spirit and speak truth to others in love.

How is God forming your identity when He asks you to speak the truth in love?

Which one do you struggle with more: truth or love?

What is one situation where you are struggling to use truth and love now?

How can you deliver the truth in love in this situation?

Day Four

Disappointments Can Become Appointments

Philippians 1:12

But I want you to know, brethren, that the things which happened to me have actually turned out for the furtherance of the gospel.

When I was twenty-two years old, I was attending a young adults' Bible study when God taught me that, if I wanted to lead others, I had to share some of my failures. Surprisingly, this was terrifying for me. I'm typically an outgoing person, but I discovered I'm also a private person, not wanting others to see my shortcomings. I was afraid that if others saw how I had failed, they would think I was not a good Christian, but that was the wrong mindset. God asked me to share so that others could learn from my mistakes and avoid the pitfalls that I succumbed to. In my sharing, I had to obey and trust God to handle how others saw me because walking in the obedience of Christ mattered more. God had to teach me that my identity was found in Him. It's not found in what others thought about me. What was important was what He thought about me, His desires for me, His praise, not that of my peers or anyone else.

Colossians 3:23 says that whatever we do we are to do it "as to the Lord and not to men." We do not want to be like the Pharisee who "loved the praise of men more than the praise of God"

(John 12:43). We want to please Him. And He desires an obedient heart; that is what makes Him smile. Not only did sharing my struggles make me relatable, oddly enough it also gave glory to God for how He brought me through the hardship and taught me life lessons. When I see God using my failures for His glory, how can I not grow confidence in sharing my faults. As Paul implies, let me boast in my weakness that God may be glorified (2 Corinthians 12:9). The things I saw as failures became opportunities for God to be glorified and allowed me to be an example and teach others. When King David repented for his sins concerning Bathsheba, he asked God to create in him a clean heart. He then asked God to teach others from his faults so that they would turn back to God also (Psalm 51:10–13). A speaker at a Voice of the Martyr's conference encouraged the audience, "Our disappointments are appointments for God." When we share our stories of how God has walked with us, we can, like Paul, boast in our weaknesses because we know who God is and who we are in Him. This is part of our identity in Christ—allowing Him to use all of us for His glory, allowing others to see Christ in every aspect of our lives.

When struggles and tribulation come, the human reaction is to be afraid, but every disappointment is an appointment from God if we will just look for the lesson before us. Paul is encouraging his fellow believers that this difficult trial (him being in prison) is bringing glory to God. It is hard to get this mindset, but Paul wants the believers to do just that—to see God in everything. Paul's desire is to spread the good news about Christ to anyone who will listen, and he wants to let his brothers and sisters in Christ know that God is using his chains for a purpose. Even when standing before King Agrippa, bound as a prisoner, Paul proclaims the goodness of God and tells the king, "I would to God that not only you, but also all who hear me today, might become both almost and altogether such as I am, except for these chains" (Acts 26:29). He would rather not be in chains, but better to be a servant of Christ in chains than a king who has not known Christ. Even when facing persecution and death, he still gives God glory.

God can use our chains and trials if we let Him. As a big sister, it is also hard to confess my failures to my younger siblings because I want them to think I am perfect. Nevertheless, I make a point to tell them so they will not falter as I did. This is how God can use our faults and setbacks to teach others. Just think, had Paul not been in prison with Silas, the jailer and his whole family would not have been saved that night (Acts 16:34). If Joseph had not been sold to Potiphar, thrown in jail, or interpreted the dreams of the servants of Pharaoh, he would never have been in a position to save his family and all of Egypt from a seven-year famine (Genesis 41–46). There is a purpose for everything under heaven, especially our trials and hardships (Ecclesiastes 3:1).

Job stands as an example of someone who lost everything and yet still remained in right standing with God, because he knew who God was (Job 1:22). He was someone who was patient through hardship and whom God abundantly blessed after the trial was over (Job 42:12–17). Trials are hard, yet they are an appointment from God for us to do or learn something. Some trials are harder than others. Job again stands as a resilient role model for those who lose loved ones, who lose position, and who lose everything that defines who they are. After losing all of his children, Job still said, "The LORD gave, and the LORD has taken away; / Blessed be the name of the LORD" (Job 1:21). That is a trial none of us want to go through, but we can remember the story of Job. We can gain strength, hope to praise and glorify God, even a peace when we have lost so much. When trials come we need to be deeply rooted in God so that we, too, can praise Him and not allow the trials to shake the roots of who we are in Him. Our identity in Christ is strengthened and sometimes founded through hardship. Take the apostles as an example. In the book of Acts, when they were beaten for their faith, they prayed for boldness and strength to continue (Acts 4:29). They were not daunted but rooted in Christ and His call. Trust God and give Him glory. Trials are only for a season; don't waste them; find God's reason and fulfill it so that your time in the drought is not wasted.

Application: Ask the Lord for eyes to see Him in the trials of life, to see the lesson in the hardship, to see His appointment in our disappointment. It is like in the book of James when we are reminded of the "perseverance of Job and [have] seen the end intended by the Lord—that the Lord is very compassionate and merciful" (James 5:11). Disappointments are appointments to learn about God, whether it be understanding how close He is willing to walk with us, seeing His grace and mercy, or watching Him fight for us, we can always learn something about Him through our struggles. God once told me to not ask to avoid the trials but to ask instead to come out victoriously. I challenge you to do the same.

How have you let the disappointments in your life define your identity?

Is there or has there been a storm in your life that has shaken you?

If so, what was it?

What have the challenges in your life taught you about God?

What have the challenging disappointments taught you about who you are in Christ?

Day Five

Unashamed

Philippians 1:20

According to my earnest expectation and hope that in nothing I shall be ashamed, but with all boldness, as always, so now also Christ will be magnified in my body, whether by life or by death.

One year, there was a guy I really, really wanted to date. But instead of asking God if he was the right one for me to date, I just asked God to please have him ask me out. So when he did, I did not ask God again if it was Christ's desire for me, I simply said yes. Overall, the date was enjoyable, but when I asked questions about his relationship with Christ, he was offended. Right then I knew it would not work out because, in order for it to work, we both needed to love God with all that we were. The truth was he didn't, but I wanted it to work so badly, even though I knew it wouldn't. I wanted to feel desirable and worth something to a man, and I wanted to date someone who lined up with God and loved Him. Those are not bad things, but to force them, to make excuses in my head, or to hope he changes is not good. To chase after someone whose identity is not in Christ is detrimental to a Christian's walk with Christ. It is important when thinking of the qualities in a person you would want to marry to want someone who has already found their identity in Christ and is living it out. I was faced with choosing between trusting God or finding my worth and identity in *if* a guy liked me or not. Needless to say, it did not work out. Not because I stopped it; no, I was hopeful. Nevertheless, God had him say no, and in that, God helped me choose to trust Him. My heart was hurt, but I hope I learned my lesson: to put my identity not in another but in God and to ask God if I am where He wants me.

Several years later God opened another relationship door, but this time I did pray. We ended up talking for three months, and we conducted ourselves in an honorable manner. And when God closed the door, neither of us had anything to be ashamed of. It was simply either the wrong time or the wrong person, nothing else. God opened that door only for a time; He was teaching me to trust Him in a new way—when everything did not make sense. I could not find my purpose, but I had to focus on Christ. Again, I had to trust God and not get so wrapped up in a relationship that I did not obey God when He chose to end it. Because God had taught me before to anchor myself in Him and His will, the young man and I were able to have no regrets in our dating relationship that would have caused shame to God or to ourselves. This is not to say it wasn't hard to trust God in the closing of another door that I too easily tried to find my identity in. It was also a test to have to reposition my identity back on Christ where it belongs. It was really hard, but when we let God and His word define us, we can be like Paul. We can live so that in everything we do, we will have no cause to be ashamed. When Christ is where our identity is rooted, we do not have to perform for others and their expectations, we just have to trust and walk with God as Jesus did. Whether it is a relationship, job, expectation, or trial, we want God to be glorified in it. We should live in a way that does not bring Him shame but in a manner that instead magnifies Him, as Paul did.

Wow, to be ashamed by nothing we have done! What a testimony! This is possible to do. Paul tells us, if we walk in the Spirit, we will not fulfill the lusts of the flesh (Galatians 5:16).

Paul has three main desires to not be ashamed of: his conduct, his boldness, and his magnification of Christ no matter the outcome. Is our devotion to Christ that strong? Or do we falter before the wicked and give up before the trial is completed? Where are we planted? Is our identity solidified in Christ so that no matter what happens we trust Him? Why do we often give up too soon? You have to answer that question yourself because I don't know what goes on inside of your head and heart. For me, I often fall because I don't ask God what He wants me to do, because I expect answers right away, or because I fear I did not hear right. But in each of these concerns, God wants me to hold on to Him, trust Him, and seek His will. He sent Christ as our example of how to live (1 Peter 2:21). Paul even says in 1 Corinthians 11:1, "Imitate me, just as I also imitate Christ." We need to be devoted like Paul. He does not care what path God takes him on, life or death. Paul's goal is to magnify Christ. He does not care what others will say or think about him, just what God will say of him at the end of time. Being made to look stupid is not even a concern for Paul. He tells the Colossians to set their minds "on things above, not on things on the earth" (Colossians 3:2).

So often we are tempted to give up because we don't like the path God has us on or what He has asked us to do. But the clay is not to argue with the Potter (Isaiah 45:9). We are instead to be moldable to God's hands and commands—willing to be obedient, wanting to magnify Him in any and every way. God is the Potter and we are the clay. The Potter has a perfect plan for the creation of every piece of clay. He sees our lump of dirt, and He sees our identity even before He begins to work on us. As God works on us throughout our lives, He is forming our identity within us. If we do argue, He can choose to allow us to do it our way, but be warned, it will not be the beautiful design that He chose for us before we were created. Which is why we want our identity to be found in Christ. Christ was obedient to the Father's touch. God is the Master Craftsmen who loved us yesterday, loves us today, and will love us tomorrow (Jeremiah 31:3). Clay is nothing but a lump without the Potter's touch. We may be required to give up all we have to follow Him, but it is worth it. The disciples chose to, and they are forever honored because of that (Luke 18:28–29). Mary, Jesus's mother, when the angel told her that she would be the mother of the Son of God, had to be willing to give up all her plans for a normal life. She knew she would have extreme trials. Joseph could have divorced her or even had her stoned if she was found with child before they were married. But she surrendered all of it, all her hopes and dreams of the quiet, peaceful, normal life and said instead that she was the Lord's handmaid and surrendered to however God wanted to shape and form her identity (Luke 1:26–38). Because of what she chose to go through for God, she is now one of the most renowned women, if not *the* most renowned woman, in all of history.

Paul was of a similar mindset that "to live is Christ, and to die is gain" (Philippians 1:21). Most of us are not there yet, but we need to be willing to walk down the path God has for us. Be bold and confident in Christ. When we stand before the Lord at the end of time we want nothing to be ashamed of and nothing left undone that He asked us to do.

Application: Pray for God to quicken your spirit that you, like Paul, may be receptive to the Lord's will, obedient to His word, and not ashamed.

What or who are you finding your identity in?

Do you feel that you give up too soon? Why?

Is there a place where you are feeling God asking you to trust Him and not to attach your identity to something or someone else?

What are you going to do about it?

Day Six

To Live

Philippians 1:21

For to me, to live is Christ, and to die is gain.

My sister asked a group of us once what was our "to live"? What were we living for? What drove our decisions and thoughts? She handed each of us a blank note card and pen—we were supposed to write it down. So I ask you the same thing: What is your "to live"? What are you living for? If you are not sure, consider where you spend your time, what hobbies you do, what you love, where you spend your money, and where you pour your energy. For Paul, what made him get up in the morning was Christ; where he spent his time, and what he spent his money on, was Christ. He tells the church at Corinth that he did not accept any money from them but preached Christ freely (2 Corinthians 11:7–9). Paul is telling us where his heart is, and we should ask ourselves where our hearts are. Mine is heavily invested in my family and relationships with people. However, my decisions should not be determined by what I think others will say or what they might think about me; my decisions must be based in Christ and Christ alone. Scripture tells me to set my affections and my mind on things above (Colossians 3:2). I should desire to get to the place where my answer can truly be as Paul's was: for me to live is Christ. Am I there? No, I am a work in progress like so many of us are, but the important part is that we recognize it and strive to overcome, try to be more like

Christ. There are days when I remember to keep my "to live" as Jesus, but it is a daily choice. I have to remember every morning to live and move with my mind set on Christ. In the book of Acts, Paul encourages us that "in Him we live and move and have our being" (Acts 17:28). Christ is our life. When our "to live" is Christ, we have freedom and can function in our proper identity as the women of God that He intended.

We really need to hone in and find our "to live" so that we can know ourselves better. What is our identity wrapped up in? It needs to be Christ. We need to keep ourselves and our desires that can cause our identity to shift in check because Christ deserves to be first in our souls. Throughout every season of our lives, our "to live" will be challenged. Peter's was. It was challenged when he denied Christ (Mark 14:70–72). It was challenged when he stood up at Pentecost before Israel and preached Christ (Acts 2). It was challenged when important Jews visited, and Paul corrected his actions (Galatians 2:11–14). It was challenged when Jesus asked him, "Do you love Me?" (John 21:15–17). And it was challenged in the storm when walking on water (Matthew 14). We will be tempted to change it, but we need to choose to stay in a mindset where our "to live" is Christ. It is vital to know that if our "to live" is anything other than Christ, then our "to die" is *not* gain.

Luke 14:26 tells us that unless we hate our family and ourselves, we are not able to be called disciples. I believe this means we cannot love anyone more than we love Christ, because in the life of a Christian we may be called to leave everyone and to give up everything in order to follow Christ. We are not to love the gifts more than the Giver. James says all good and perfect gifts come from above, from God (James 1:17). So our love for Him should be greater than our love for what He has given us. It is not that we do not love them, but in contrast to our love of God, it is like a dim light. Our love for family and friends is to pale in comparison so greatly that it would look as though we hated them because it does not compare with how we are to love God. If we love others or other things more than Christ, then we will be reluctant to obey God, which is sin. Matthew 16:25 says if we desire to save our lives, we will lose them, but if we give them up willingly, we will gain them.

There is so much more than what is in this life; eternity awaits us. But we must be willing to lay down this life. The disciples were called to leave their nets (Mark 1:18). Many brothers and sisters in other countries are called to literally leave everyone and everything they love. Their commitment to Christ must be top priority. Peter was asked by Jesus, "Do you love Me more than these?" (John 21:15). Now this could mean more than the other disciples. What if Christ was asking if Peter loved Him more than the material things of life, fishing and nets, his livelihood, his hobbies? Do we love Christ more than our livelihood, families, and friends? Scripture tells us if we love Him, we will obey Him (John 14:15). If God says to leave those people and things behind and follow Him, will we do it? Sometimes we think God will call others to do those things, leave their families to be missionaries, but not us. Watch out. Christ wants to be our "to live," and nothing can compete with Him. He is a jealous God, not wanting any other gods before Him, in a good way (Exodus 20:3–5). He wants to be whom our identity is found in; He made us. He might just ask us to do something not because He is against us but to test us and grow us in our surrender, trust, and love for Him. After Jesus asked Peter if he loved Him more than these, Christ gave Peter something to do: feed His flock. Do we love Him more than our "to live"? I am not there yet and likely neither are you, but God willing, one day we will get there. We can only get to that place where our "to live" becomes Christ when our identity is solid in Him, when we lean on Him, the One who strengthens us (Philippians 4:13).

The contrast of my "to live" for me or "to live" for Christ can be easily paired with dating relationships. Too often, especially where the heart is involved, we date someone and allow our "to live" to become our godly boyfriend. We put him first and value his opinion above all others. God becomes a close second. If we are not careful, we can even get to the point where we think we cannot live without him. What if God called you to surrender that desire and give up that dream? How could we possibly give him up? We must be willing to lay aside everything for God. No other gods before Him includes hopes and dreams. This is a serious situation. If we ever find ourselves getting to that point where our relationship with someone is rivaling our relationship with God, we unconsciously announce what our "to live" is. That means it is not God. God is a jealous God, and there will be no others before Him, not even a godly Mr. Perfect (Exodus 20:3–5). When God chooses to close the door or take something or someone away, we have to trust Him. Our hearts may be broken and shattered because we placed our identity in a human rather than God, but we are not abandoned. God has not left us alone. Christ is mercifully there to pick up the pieces of our shattered hearts. When a relationship that is out of God's order ends, we have to refind ourselves in God. This can happen with dating couples, widows, or anyone who puts their identity into someone other than God. When that "someone else" is gone, we think that is the end, but it is not because Christ is waiting to be our "to live," and He has work for us to do. You see, God does not want us to have any other gods before Him (Exodus 20:3), so He will try to pry them away until we see Him for who He is and choose to place Him in His rightful place in our lives. Don't fight against God when He closes doors or removes things or people from your life. Trust Him. It is so much easier if we surrender them now and live for Christ today than to fight and hurt ourselves later.

Application: Pray and ask God, What is your "to live"? What is it that makes you tick and consumes or fills your thoughts and heart? Now ask your Savior to teach you to have Christ as your "to live" instead of whatever it is that you are living for. May He give you the strength to surrender and lay aside your plans for His.

How does living for Christ define who you are and solidify your identity?

What is your "to live"?

What are all your decisions based off of?

If we are not living for God, how can we change that? What do we need to do differently?

Week One Overview

What did God teach you about your identity this week?

Where is our true identity found?

What can we try to place our identity in?

How do struggles create our identity?

Day Seven

One Mind

Philippians 1:27

Only let your conduct be worthy of the gospel of Christ, so that whether I come and see you or am absent, I may hear of your affairs, that you stand fast in one spirit, with one mind striving together for the faith of the gospel.

When my siblings and I helped my sister and brother-in-love build their house, a Quonset hut, we each had a role to fulfill for the accomplishment of a great task. This house is made of metal arches, like a crescent moon, that all fit together. My brother was the anchor to steady the structure as we raised the huge arches in place. Two others were on scaffolding pulling the arches with ropes, which they would remove once the arch was in place and then connect the pieces together at the top. The rest of us were ground crew. We started by lifting the arch all at once, giving the leverage my brother needed to begin pulling. Then we were to stabilize each wobbly arch with two-by-four boards until it was in place. Two members of the ground crew had an additional job to hold down the two ends and bolt them into the keyways so that the arch would keep shape and not flap around dangerously and cut someone. Every role was essential to the completion of the project. No one job was more important than the other. Everyone was needed. We did not complain about which position we had. It was not a matter of who was the greatest but that each of us used what God has given us to help one another. We did not lose our individuality but vectored it for the greater purpose of one common goal. If we had not been of one mind, the job would never have been completed; someone could have gotten seriously injured, and we would not have accomplished a magnificent task. But we did work together and saw the fruit of our labor. As we connected the arches together, they became stronger and able to withstand more and more pressure. Once we had three arches up, they were supposed to be able to withstand a hurricane. The body of Christ is like that—we are stronger together. With three or more, God has promised to be in the midst, and we will be able to stand (Matthew 18:20).

While we stand fast, we are to strive to conduct ourselves in a manner that portrays and parallels what the gospel teaches. We are called to love the Lord with all our heart, soul, mind, and strength and to love our neighbor as ourselves (Mark 12:30–31). We are to take up our cross and follow Christ and His example (Matthew 16:24). Basically, we are to practice what we preach and live as Christians who have been set free. Also, Paul instructs us to be unified. With so much division going on in our world today, unification would stand out like a sore thumb, hopefully drawing people to Christ. "God is not the author of confusion but of peace" (1 Corinthians 14:33). And He wants His people unified with the mind of Christ. God's people are not supposed to look like the world. Romans 12:2 says, "Do not be conformed to this world, but be transformed by the renewing of your mind." Being of one mind is a miracle in humanity, only accomplished through the strength of the Holy Spirit and the fear of the Lord. We are to be in the world but not of the world (John 17:16). In order to accomplish this, we must set our identity in Christ, to be used for His purposes. Like building the house, we each had our own individual jobs, but we were unified in our work as one body. Now, being unified does not mean we lose our identity. A toe is still a toe when it is connected to the rest of the body. The hand, foot, and toe each are individual but when united they can do so much more. When our identity is in Christ and not in the world, we strengthen the body of Christ and draw others to Him through our example.

When Jesus was in the garden, He prayed for unification among the believers that we would draw others to know God (John 17:21). This unification begins in the families of Christians. From there, it moves to our churches, to our communities, to our cities, to our states, to our nation, and then to the world! It is like the Great Commission from the book of Acts: we are to be His witnesses first in Jerusalem, then Judea and Samaria, and then to the ends of the earth (Acts 1:8). Our families are our Jerusalem. Unifying the family is possible; it can be challenging but still possible. When I was growing up, there were ten kids in the house. So if unifying us was possible, anything is! Unifying our motley crew was quite a challenge for Mom and Dad, I am sure, but if we could be united, so can you. Unification—working together for a common cause; one mind and ready to work—is challenging but beautiful. However, in ourselves we argue that we want to be individuals, not one unit. We don't want to be lost in the crowd. We have our own ideas, our own parts to contribute, our own plans. Unification does not take away identity or individuality. It builds off of it and incorporates each part for the greater good of God's plan. God's desire is that the body of Christ be His body and act like it. There is only one body, but it has many different working parts. Under whose mind are we united though? Not yours and not mine, but God's. Christ is the head of the church (Ephesians 5:23 and Colossians 1:18).

If we are all striving to follow Christ and find our identity in Him, then as the head, He will guide the rest of the body to work together. Each part has a different function, yet it is one body working together, in unison for a common cause. Feet are for walking. Eyes are for seeing. Fingers and hands are for touching others in the service of Christ. A mouth proclaims the wonders of God and encourages others. A heart pumps life into all the body encouraging one another as we move together. Shoulders carry burdens and support the head. Knees support us and bow before our lord as prayer warriors. Arms carry heavy loads. Legs run the race of endurance. Toes support the feet. Ears hear. Scripture tells us, in the book of Ephesians, that Christ is the head "from whom the whole body, joined and knit together by what every joint supplies, according to the effective working by which every part does its share, causes growth of the body for the edifying of itself in love" (Ephesians 4:16). Everything is to support the other in the service of God, and we are challenged to be content in the position of life God has given us. We are still individuals because Christ made us unique to His good pleasure, but we are unified with one purpose and one mind.

Application: Pray and ask for a mind of humility—the mind of Christ—so that we may be united under the direction of Christ and not our own will.

How do we still move in our own identity but be united with others in one mindset?

Where has God placed you? What has He given you to do?

Whose mind should we have?

Day Eight

The Mind of Suffering

Philippians 1:29

For to you it has been granted on behalf of Christ, not only to believe in Him, but also to suffer for His sake.

My pastor once said, "God did not come to make us happy. He came to make us holy." Suffering can be part of the purification process. One day I was outside crying to God because the status I wanted to define me of becoming a wife and mother was being delayed and altogether stopped. I did not want to give up this dream and future identity, but God asked me to do just that and submit to His current plan for my life. Wasn't a good girl supposed to be rewarded with the desires of her heart? That would be nice, but life is not always as we imagine or plan. My desires needed to be refined. I was making the dream of wife and mother my identity when what I truly needed was to make Christ my identity. What He asked and desired of me was for me to trust Him with my identity. God had some purification in mind to take me deeper than I had walked before. This life is not about the rewards God gives; it is about loving, serving, and obeying God. He taught me that as I let go of what I wanted and chose to place my identity in Him and trust Him with His plan for who He wanted me to be, I would learn to become more like His Son and to love Him more. When we love God without demands, we can more easily see the beauty of His plan. He also taught me that through suffering He is purifying and making me holy. On the swing in a garden area outside the front of our house, I read in the Bible the words "Be holy, for I am holy" (1 Peter 1:16). Before then, I never thought it possible to strive and achieve holiness. But on that summer day, it hit me: If God calls us to be holy, then it is possible. However, like everything else great and good, holiness comes with a cost, as mentioned above.

We have been given the privilege to suffer for His name's sake; it has been granted to us. What a different way of looking at things. Christ said, "If they persecuted Me, they will also persecute you" (John 15:20). Suffering is just a fulfillment of the word of God. It does not take away our identity; it enhances it. Suffering builds character. "Tribulation produces perseverance; and perseverance, character; and character, hope" (Romans 5:3–4). We are to bear it with endurance as Christ did, with submission and a moldable heart. Hebrews tells us that for the joy set before Him, He endured the cross (Hebrews 12:2). Matthew says those who are persecuted are blessed for they inherit the kingdom of God (Matthew 5:10–12). Why is it so hard for us to accept that suffering is a part of our inheritance? When we are slighted, shunned, or persecuted for our beliefs and how we live our lives—our identity in Christ—we need to train our minds to understand that this is normal for believers. The world did all these things to Christ, and if they did it to Him, we can assume that the world will do this to us also (John 15:20). We should not collapse or cave in; we should trust God to be with us and walk on with Him. Know that others have experienced these things and allow their stories to inspire and guide you to holiness. The writer of Hebrews tells us of those in the faith who, in scripture, walked before us (Hebrews 11). And James tells us to "take the prophets . . . as an example of suffering and patience" (James 5:10), for they go hand in hand. Realizing that suffering is part of our inheritance is part of having the mind of Christ, and enduring through it is the action of Christ. It is contrary to the world, but that is because the world has no part of God. One reason we can rejoice in suffering is because we are counted worthy to partake in the suffering of Christ. The apostles did this in Acts 4 and 5. We are partakers with Him and joint heirs (Romans 8:17). Persecution should be expected. Suffering is like the trademark of the family. They beat and persecuted Him, so of course the world will hate and persecute us (John 15:18). For example, I not only have the last name of Hagel but also look a lot like my sisters, so if someone was mad at my sisters they might also be mad at me because we are related. Hopefully by how I act, people can know that I am both a Christian and a Hagel. If someone does not like one of my sisters for any reason, I will feel their displeasure because I am with her, look like her, and am related to her. When one of us gets judged by society, we all do. For example, when one of us did well in a college class, the instructors expected us all to excel in the subject even though we did not have the same major. In my sophomore year in college, I took a required upper-level English class, and I was worried because this instructor had taught two of my older siblings who were both English majors. I was not an English major and wondered if he would hold me to the high standard that they set before me. As Christians, we have a name to uphold. The word *Christian* is based on the word *Christ*. We are to both bear His name and resemble his life. Therefore, if we look like Christ, the world will expect us to be like Him and hate us simply because they hated Him (John 15:18–25). But our identity is not found on or in this world. As Christians, our identity is solidified in Christ. What the world thinks or does doesn't matter. What matters is what God thinks. How can we live in a manner that reflects Christ in our day-to-day life, no matter what persecutions come our way?

In college my older sister was one year ahead of me, and she challenged a book that was required in her class. We were at a Christian college, but the book that the class was requiring her to read promoted the worst of morals, all through it. It made grown men and women blush due to the content. When she stood up and contested the book, she was persecuted. The instructor and the dean of the school, both men, had a private meeting with her and challenged this young woman for stating that the book did not uphold the Christian standards proclaimed by the school on their policy regarding no porn on campus. She was merely asking to read a different book, but they would not allow it. If she did not complete the reading, my sister would receive an F on the midterm. Therefore, her choices were to take an F or drop the class (which was required for her major). She chose to drop the class. When asked what she would do when having to take the class again for her major, she steadfastly declared that she would change majors, if necessary. That book was not something any young Christian adult should have to be exposed to. She was a junior at this point. This is not a story where everyone was convicted and did the right thing; no, she dropped the class halfway through, which meant she did not even get a refund. However, God did use her standing up to change the curriculum a year later for other students, which did result in the removal of the book. When we place our identity in Christ and our love for Him, no matter the persecution, we set an example and allow God to use us for His glory (even if it hurts and even if we do not see the example we set).

Being persecuted is the privilege of being in the family of God. I know that sounds odd to our human ears, but when we are persecuted we can rejoice because we have been counted as one of His and found worthy to suffer for Christ (Acts 5:41). This was something I often reminded myself of when I went through a relationship trial. There was a guy I thought I wanted to date, but he mocked me for my faith and my standards on our first coffee date. When the door closed, I repeatedly thanked God for counting me worthy to be stretched by Him. I dare not count that as persecution compared to others who truly live and die for Christ, but I did repeat that to myself in order to get my mind to be thankful for the heart's disappointment. When our identity is not in Christ, life's trials and persecutions can cause us great oppression, anxiety, and distress. We don't see the good God is doing in us. However, when our identity is placed in Christ and those trials, sufferings, and persecutions arise, we can see them as opportunities to be faithful to God as Christ was, to endure for the glory of the cross. We are His. Because of our endurance through suffering we are counted as heirs to the kingdom of God! Is it not worth it to go through a little temporary pain and suffering now for the joy that will come after? Jesus thought so (Hebrews 12:2).

Application: Pray that when persecution arises, God will give you the grace and strength to rejoice in Him and to live like the example of Christ.

How does God use suffering in our lives to shape us as women of God?

How does suffering strengthen the identity He has designed in our lives?

What should our mindset be toward suffering?

What are some Bible verses about suffering?

Who is one person you know who has walked through suffering?

What is their story, and what can you learn from it?

Day Nine

Being Unified

Philippians 2:2

Fulfill my joy by being like-minded, having the same love, being of one accord, of one mind.

Being unified starts with submission. I have had the opportunity to practice this recently. My parents chose to be humble and endure a recent injustice done to them, but I wanted to fight for them. When I appealed, they still believed God wanted our family to endure this rather than stand up and fight it. I could have argued and taken action myself, but that would not have been living in one accord. Scripture tells me I am to honor my parents (Exodus 20:12). So I also chose to humble myself and pray. I pray that God will make it clear to them when it is time to stop the injustice, but until then, I pray that He will strengthen us to endure with peace and joy.

I have also had the opportunity to practice submission in a relationship where I wanted to move forward, but God showed Himself to have other plans for me. There was a young man who wanted to date me and I him, but Dad and Mom did not have peace about the two of us dating at that time. We prayed for two months but still no peace on their end. Because my parents are my spiritual authority, and God was still withholding His peace even with all the sincere praying, I had to believe that it was God's will for me not to date this young man. So even though I did not see it or understand it, my choice was and is to trust God and walk in submission to His will and His guidance through submission to my parents. As time passed, I was able to see that we would not have blessed each other in our walks with the Lord. We were both walking with God, but He had different paths for us. We were not a match, but I could only see that after submission and surrendering my will to God's will.

Submission is a key attribute to finding our identity in Christ. Submission to God does not take away our identity; it enhances it. God has created each one of us; He formed us and knit us together in our mothers' wombs (Psalm 139:13 and Jeremiah 1:5). He created each of us for "such a time as this" (Esther 4:14). He has a plan and a purpose for us that is much greater than we could ever know, and we each have a role in His plan. But to fulfill that role properly, we must humble ourselves and submit ourselves to God's authority.

As women, God has protected us through our fathers or our spouses as spiritual heads through whom we trust God to work. Scripture also guides us toward this when it talks about children honoring their parents and wives submitting to their husbands (Ephesians 5:22–6:9). God made husbands and fathers as the head of the family to care for and protect those under their authority (Ephesians 5:23–24). This does not mean we cannot hear God for ourselves, but it is a safeguard when we are not sure what God's will is. Through God's sovereignty and grace, we have someone above us to talk to and counsel us. Also, by trusting God to work through our authorities, it creates unity in the family and, perhaps more important, humility within us, which is a characteristic of Christ. As we submit to God through humbling ourselves to our spiritual authority, we are developing and finding our identity with Christ. Remember, even Christ submitted Himself to His parents when His mother asked Him to help with the wedding feast at Cana, and He did His first recorded miracle (John 2:1–11).

The book of Philippians is all about having the mindset of Christ. Paul is telling them to be of one mind, to be the body, to be the church. In verse 3 of chapter 2, Paul describes what this mindset is to look like. It is to be unified, to choose to have the mind of Christ. I had to choose to be unified with my family against the wrong being done to them, as much as I did not want to, because, ultimately, a house divided will not stand (Matthew 12:25). Unity, especially in today's world, is almost nonexistent, therefore it makes what Paul is teaching powerful, relevant, and extraordinary. That is also why unity in the body of Christ is so vital now. Life is too much like the rat race where we all watch out for number one, where everyone's ideas are accepted no matter how outlandish or wrong, and then acted upon. Our society in America is a place where individualism is praised to the point of division in our nation. Even within individual political parties, there is disunity. Paul was concerned that Christians would fall prey to disunity; he wrote, "I plead with you, brethren, by the name of our Lord Jesus Christ, that you all speak the same thing, and that there be no divisions among you, but that you be perfectly joined together in the same mind and in the same judgment" (1 Corinthians 1:10). We are not to "be conformed to this world" (Romans 12:2). We are to let the light of Christ shine in us (Matthew 5:16). That is what makes Christians so unique: there is to be unity in God's family and in the house of God. We do not lose our individualism and identity but apply it to the cause of Christ. Instead of insisting on our own way, the knitting together of our individuality makes a beautiful body of Christ. One is the foot, another is the arm, someone is the hand, another the heart, and on it goes. We should never wish to be someone else, because God uniquely designed each of us to be united for His purposes and His kingdom.

If we can work unity into our churches, I believe it will be a great witnessing tool, because the unification of that many people is astronomical. How does this happen? It begins in the home and family, then it spills over into the churches and then into the towns, and on and on. One of Paul's requirements for deacons to Timothy is that the deacon's children be under control, in unity and submission to their father (1 Timothy 3:11–12). Paul gives the church steps for unity in the family. By having a godly leader with direction, the family can be guided as one unit for God. Women, you as the helpmates have a crucial role in creating this unity. Moms make the house run either for Dad or against him. You and your husband need to be on the same page spiritually in how you raise your children. Even if one of the ideas is wrong for the family, you need to submit to each other and hear what God is telling the other parent; pray about it (Ephesians 5:21). As you both pray over the path, God will direct it, and as long as both are in submission to God and to each other, then God will make your paths straight. Wives, if your husband, after praying, still believes where God is leading the family is the opposite direction from what you think, then you be the vector by putting yourself behind him and praying the whole way. Trust that God can move mountains, so if your husband or parent(s) is hearing wrong, trust that God can move them as you remain in submission to God and your spiritual leader. You submit to the authority that God has placed over you in obedience to Christ and pray hard that God lead through him. Wives are called by God and instructed by Paul to submit to their husbands (Ephesians 5:22). That is when we say, "OK, God, I don't understand, but You have placed this man as the head of our family so I will follow." Then we pray hard that God puts us, as a unified family, on the road He wants us on or stops us from heading down the wrong way. In this way, we guide the family in obedience and support of where God is leading the family as a whole through the head. When both the man and the woman are truly seeking God, God in His mercy will guide them together—"Seek, and you will find" is what scripture tells us (Matthew 7:7). It is not a matter of trusting the man; it is a matter of trusting God to lead through him.

As for unmarried women, it is vital that we submit ourselves to the authority, protection, and wisdom of the parents God has placed in our lives. Scripture is full of reminders for children (and this does not just mean little kids) to honor and listen to their parents. Proverbs 1:8 says, "Hear the instruction of your father, and do not forsake the law of your mother." And Proverbs 23:22 tells us, "Listen to your father who begot you, and do not despise your mother when she is old." This is not a caution to a young child but counsel for an adult child. Regarding unity in the house in respect to the children, we are called to honor and obey our parents. This is "the first commandment with promise" (Ephesians 6:1–3). As long as we are in their house we need to submit to our parents and pray for them that God keeps them on the right track for our family. Submission is a lot about prayer, and unity is a lot about trusting God. Parents are the core of the family unity. It begins with each in submission to God and to one another. In the book of Ephesians, Paul calls us "to walk worthy of the calling with which [we] were called, with all lowliness and gentleness, with longsuffering, bearing with one another in love, endeavoring to keep the unity of the Spirit in the bond of peace" (Ephesians 4:1–3).

What if the person I am submitting to is stubborn? Don't worry. God can use a donkey (Numbers 22:21–39). In the book of Numbers a man named Balaam wanted to disobey God. He begged the Lord to get his own way and, when God relented, the man rode his donkey to his destination. But the Lord was angry at Balaam's decision and lack of humility. He sent an angel to kill this disobedient soul. Nevertheless, God allowed the donkey to save the man's life by speaking to him, then God opened Balaam's eyes to see what God had intended. When the man realized what was about to happen, he humbled himself and submitted to the will of God (Numbers 22:31–34). God regained the man's obedience. If God can use a donkey, He can use a human.

Application: Unity begins with submission. Pray for a submissive attitude toward God and those He has put over you. Pray for discernment so you will know whom God expects you to submit to and then pray for them to be led by God. Even Jesus told the Jews that the Pharisees sat on the seat of Moses and so the Jews should do what they said, but they should not do what they did (Matthew 23:1–3).

How does trusting God for unity help us find our identity in Christ?

What is one area where God is calling you to trust and submit to Him?

What is stopping you from obeying?

Is there someone you are having trouble being unified with?

What is causing the disunity?

How can it be fixed?

Day Ten

Love Others

Philippians 2:3

Let nothing be done through selfish ambition or conceit, but in lowliness of mind let each esteem others better than himself.

When I was little, I loved to serve supper. So much so that when someone else tried to serve, I would protest in my childish voice, "Let me serve you!" While this pales in comparison to what Paul is teaching and was not the most respectful response, I think my parents let me get away with it because it was the beginning steps to esteeming others better than myself in order to serve them. Almost thirty years have passed since then, and I still like to serve supper. I just enjoy it because I enjoy serving others, helping others, and I can make sure everyone has enough to eat. This is a good thing, but if I am not careful, I can get so wrapped up in my being the one who serves supper that I fail in letting others have a turn to grow in their service. Then it becomes all about me and how I view myself. I can let my identity as a servant consume my mind and think I am only someone if I am always in the middle of things and serving. However, if my goal becomes "I have to serve them," then it loses the heart of what Paul is saying. I am making it about me when Paul says to always consider others before yourself. For instance, another lesson I learned when very young was to never take the last piece of food on the plate without asking everyone else if they would like it first. This, again, was to teach young children to be considerate of others before thinking of themselves, to not be selfish but kind and thoughtful.

This fulfills the second-greatest commandment. Jesus tells us the first and greatest commandment is to love God with all that we are and the second is to love people as ourselves (Matthew 22:36–40). God's Word constantly leads back to the same point. We are to care for and serve others, but we must always keep God first. We cannot let our love for anything else trump our love and devotion to God. Put God first, and He will help everything else fall into its proper place into the identity you were created for. "Commit your works to the LORD, and your thoughts will be established" (Proverbs 16:3). The Philippians (I believe) already had great love for Christ, and for Paul, but Paul was reminding them of the mindset they needed to constantly live in toward others, putting others before themselves. This is not fake humility that Paul is encouraging; he is reminding them how to live as Christ. Would you want to know what Christ thought, what He meditated on? Paul clearly tells us in this letter that humility is the mindset of Christ, not thinking of Himself but of the Father, how to obey the will of God. Verses 5 through 8 in this chapter talk about Christ being equal with God but humbling Himself and coming down to earth as a human. While He was in the form of a human, He humbled Himself still further to the will of the Father and was obedient to die on the cross; the most torturous death at that time (Philippians 2:5–8).

Paul told us, "To live is Christ" (Philippians 1:21). Jesus is the example and the standard we ought to try to reach while living here on this earth. He says, "Be holy, for I am holy" (1 Peter 1:16). This is a common theme throughout this book, to have the mind of Christ. It ought to grow like fruit on the vine so that as we live, Christ dwells and lives and moves within us. This is good fruit. Scripture says, in Acts 17:28, "In Him we live and move and have our being." He is whom our lives revolve around.

In Him we live. In Him is our identity. But to be in Him we have to be like Him and humble ourselves to be obedient to the will of the Father that we may let His light shine before us, that we should want everything we say and do to bring glory to God and point others to Him. But all too often we get caught up in ourselves and how others will see us. We think our identity is based on their opinions. The result is we take our eyes off God. We all know what happened to Peter when he walked on water but took his eyes off Jesus; Peter began to sink. Just moments before, he was walking on water, but when he was distracted by what was going on around him, his eyes slipped off of Christ, and he began to be engulfed in the sea (Matthew 14:22–32). The world is full of distractions. Distractions are dangerous and can be detrimental. They cause us to doubt God and think that He is not enough. We think our identity needs more than Christ, and we begin to listen to the wind and waves. We become worried and afraid. But scripture tells us that if we lack wisdom all we have to do is ask God for it (James 1:5). When Peter was falling, he cried out to God, and God was right there for him. Jesus said, "Ask, and it will be given to you" (Matthew 7:7). He also taught us to "seek first the kingdom of God" (Matthew 6:33). So if we desire the mind of Christ, then we should ask. We can begin right now by humbling ourselves and becoming obedient to the will and Word of God.

Application: Pray for humility that God would teach us to humble ourselves in His sight so that we may be like Christ.

How does serving others shape who we are in Christ?

How can we love others better?

Who is someone God is calling you to serve?

Why should we serve others?

Day Eleven

Walking in the Mind of Christ

Philippians 2:5

Let this mind be in you which was also in Christ Jesus.

Getting into this mindset is a difficult task. One year my sisters and I successfully put on a young adults' conference, but after it was finished my analysis of it had a gray lens over it, a fog that I saw it through because it was not as impactful, I felt, as the one before. Because of my view, I did not want to do the conference the next year. But literally, God told me through others, twice in one day, that we still needed to plan to do the conference for Him the following year even though I did not want to. He brought confirmation in accordance with His will. My job was to obey. Amazingly, within one day, He even used two random people to ask me about when the next conference would be. After the second person asked, God said, "Do you need another?" So we began planning. I had to lay aside my personal thoughts and look at this conference through the lens of obedience to God, which is the mindset of Christ. As we approached the conference the next year, one of my prayer partners asked what to pray for. I asked her to pray that I would be able to see what God was doing. I needed to see with His eyes and not through gray, depressing lenses. Unknowingly I was asking her to pray that I have the eyes and mind of Christ. God did answer her and my prayers, and I not only got to see the conference clearly through His eyes but He also brightened the previous year as well. I had gotten wrapped up in how I wanted the conference to feel, what I wanted others to see, and I had missed God's purpose. I felt like if the conference did not obtain the physical achievements from the year before, it was wasted. I had wrapped up my identity, my achievements, in the conference of my mind and not that of God's mind. We cannot let our identity get caught up in our definition of success. Success comes from God. If anything brings God glory, it is not wasted. He has a plan far greater than we can ever imagine. Throughout Christ's earthly ministry, He constantly implied that He came to glorify the Father (John 12:28; 13:31; 17:1). We, too, are made to glorify the Father, and He is glorified when we walk as Christ walked. When I surrendered to Christ's mindset, I could finally see the true beauty that He had made and how He was glorified in it.

Paul goes on to describe the mind of Christ, but let's just focus on the phrase "the mind of Christ" for a little bit longer. Jesus told His disciples how He only did and said what He saw the Father doing and heard the Father saying (John 5:19). He was in such communion with God that He heard God's heart constantly. His thoughts and His desires were to obey the Father. Jesus knew, as Samuel told King Saul, "To obey is better than sacrifice" (1 Samuel 15:22–23). Christ was obedient to serve others, preach, do miracles, and even die on the cross, all as the Father led (Philippians 2:7).

We may not understand why God is asking us to do some things or walk through something hard, but here is where we trust in His sovereignty and goodness; we choose to be like Christ, obeying no matter what. Here is where our identity is truly formed. Like coal being formed into a diamond, it is in the pressure and heat of harder times that we bring out who we really are. But we may still ask why God is doing this, why we trust Him in these difficult times. Because God is the One who designed us, and He is the One who defines us. He sends us through hardships to bring our identity more in line with His image, to show the world His work that He may be glorified. When we walk in the mindset of Christ, we allow Him to do this, and it brings glory to God just as Jesus did so many times. Christ was obedient not to heal the man at the gate Beautiful. Yes, I said Christ was obedient to refrain from healing someone. The man at the gate Beautiful was lame and sat at the entrance of the temple for many years; don't you think Jesus passed him regularly? Jesus went to the temple all the time, but that man was not for Him to heal, he was for Peter and John to heal after the death and resurrection of Jesus (Acts 3:1–8). This showed the power and glory of Christ beyond His death and resurrection, and oh, by the way, it kind of proved His resurrection to the people of that time, and it was a signal to the world that Jesus is Lord! God wanted Peter and John to do it, so Christ did not heal the man. Sometimes when we are on a "Jesus high" we want to touch everyone, but we also want to hear "Well done, good and faithful servant" (Matthew 25:23). Therefore, we must listen closely to know what the will of God is, to know whom to touch and whom not to. We must obey the word of God. Jesus said, "If you love Me, keep My commandments" (John 14:15). There are some who will come in the end times and say, "Lord, Lord have we not prophesied in Your name, cast out demons in Your name?" And He will say to them, "Depart from Me, you who practice lawlessness" (Matthew 7:23). What? Does that seem confusing? Keep searching the Scriptures. It is not about what we have done, our good works; God is after our hearts and souls, so it is more about how we obey Him, how we love Him, and how we allow our identity to be found and formed in Him, not in what we want to do but in what He wants us to do.

What has God asked you to do? I confess I do not always obey every time, right away. There are times we don't obey because we are afraid (like the servant with the one talent who, when the Master entrusted him with it, did nothing with it except bury it in the ground [Matthew 25:18]). Instead we should make it our goal to obey the first time. Too often I have not found myself in this immediate obedience category. For example, if God wants me to talk to someone I don't know, I might delay. I am anxious about what strangers will think of me if I just start talking to them about God. Most people who know me would not think I have any issues with this because I am happy to talk to just about anyone, but I do still have a hard time breaking the ice in a conversation to a totally unknown person. But when I put aside the fear I have, obey the nudge that God gives, and trust Him, I step into the identity that I know God has built in me. And when I obey, He does things. Sometimes it is randomly praying for someone in the middle of the store, sometimes it is making a new friend, or sometimes it is just encouraging someone. God wants us to do what He has asked the first time because He has a plan, and He wants to allow us to be a part of it. If we choose to disobey, His plan will still come to fruition but through someone else. Esther is a perfect example. Mordecai tells her that she must go before the king to save her people. Now this could have easily cost her life. Mordecai tells her that if she does not do this (due to fear), God will deliver the Jews through someone else, but she would surely die (Esther 4:14). Even though her future was unknown and frightening, Esther obeyed and God saved the Jews. God knows what is best, so why do we fight so hard against obeying Him? We should fight against disobedience if we are to have the mind of Christ, one where we only say and do what the Father is saying and doing. May God give us the courage and grace to have the mind of Christ.

Application: Pray for obedience that will move us to respond in submission and obedience to the will of the Father. Now be prepared to practice obedience. Opportunities will arise because God often helps us learn through circumstances and situations that will challenge us to act upon what we prayed for.

How does walking in the mind of Christ bring out the truth of our identity; what is etched inside us?

Describe what happens to you when the mind of Christ is etched inside you.

What has God asked you to do?

What are you going to do about it?

What is stopping you from obeying?

Day Twelve

Our Humble Savior

Philippians 2:7

But [Christ] made Himself of no reputation, taking the form of a bondservant, and coming in the likeness of men.

This is one of my favorite verses in the entire Bible because it shows the humility of Jesus, a beautiful picture of how we, too, should live our lives. At every church God has called us to, our family tries to plug in serving somewhere. We will wash the dishes, serve drinks, take out the trash, basically do anything we can to help. My parents taught us to take humble jobs in order to be able to serve God anywhere and everywhere. This may not be the way you imagined serving God, but He is glorified in the little and big acts of service. So often we can get caught up in wanting to do the big things, thinking that somehow it is more important. It is too easy to lose ourselves, our identity, to what others think. We want others to see us and acknowledge our service, at least too often I do. But Christ does not identify with the proud and boastful but with the humble. If we want to be identified with Christ then we need to become like the lowly and serve where He asks. Scripture warns that those who humble themselves will be exalted and those who exalt themselves will be humbled (Luke 14:11). The book of Proverbs tells us before honor comes humility (Proverbs 18:12). That does not have to be humiliation, just humility. Mom and Dad wanted to teach their children to serve as Christ did, with humility. When you and I choose to serve others through the lowly jobs, even the ones no one wants, we are exhibiting the character of Christ.

Think about this for a moment: the God of the entire universe, so much above us, came down to be one of us, to serve. The Almighty, who held back His full power when breathing into Adam (so not to combust him), came as a helpless baby. The star breather of the heavens made Himself shrink to our level so that He could save us. According to Isaiah, we are like grasshoppers to the Lord (Isaiah 40:22). That would be like a human (if we could) turning himself into a grasshopper to save their species from eternal extinction and damnation. We are so inferior to Him, yet He humbled Himself to walk with us as a man. And He didn't just become a man; He became a baby. We human beings are pitiful enough, but an infant can do nothing for himself. He came, from the right hand of the throne in heaven, to be a baby in a manger, where He could not feed Himself, dress Himself, change Himself, or even talk for Himself. That is how downgraded Jesus became out of obedience to the Father and love for us. What humility! He gave it all up and then was ridiculed, beaten, and crucified by these "grasshoppers" whom He came to save. That is what our Jesus did to set us free from sin. This is what He endured to glorify God. This is the mind of Christ, our humble Savior, to become nothing but an obedient servant to a holy and compassionate God. The prophet Isaiah and the book of Matthew describe Him as humble, meek, and the One who will not break a broken reed. He is one who will not revile nor shout in the streets in anger (Matthew 12:19–20). He is our example to be humble by choice in body, speech, and spirit.

The other part of Philippians 2:7 says that Jesus became a bondservant. What is a bondservant? That was a slave who, at the time of liberation, chose to forever remain a slave to their master. This act of devotion was an example of what an amazing master one had. Jesus Christ, our Lord and Savior, chose to submit to God, whom He was equal with, and allow God to be His Master. Servants were identified by who their master was—Hagar to Sarai, Gehazi to Elisha (Genesis 16:1 and 25:12; 2 Kings 4:12). Moses, the great leader and deliverer of Israel from Egypt, was called "Moses the servant of the Lord" (Joshua 12:6; Deuteronomy 34:5). Paul taught Timothy that "a servant of the Lord must not quarrel but be gentle to all" (2 Timothy 2:24). Jesus taught His disciples "if anyone desires to be first, he shall be last of all and servant of all" (Mark 9:35). He was teaching them the importance of humility. God is an awesome Master. If Christ, who is His equal, chooses to humble Himself, obey and serve God, how much more should we, tiny grasshoppers, choose to humble ourselves and trust and obey God also?

Application: Pray: Lord, help us to have the humility and submission of Christ. He emptied Himself for Your glory. Please give us the grace and strength to do the same.

How does humility shape our identity in Christ?

How do we grow our humility?

What does Christ teach us about how to be humble?

Where can we serve God with humility?

Week Two Overview

What did God teach you about your identity this week?

Describe being of one mind.

How do suffering and humility work in defining our identity?

How are loving and serving others part of finding our identity in Christ?

Day Thirteen

The Humble Mind of Obedience

Philippians 2:8

And being found in appearance as a man, He humbled Himself and became obedient to the point of death, even the death of the cross.

When my little brother began to grow astronomically with God, my heart swelled with great joy. This was not because I did anything to make it happen; it was because he was gaining the mind of Christ, applying it to his life, and being humble. He began to take correction better, to listen more, to serve more. His entire mindset, mannerisms, and choices changed. Don't get me wrong, he was a good kid before, but there was an obvious difference in identity. Most of us can say the same when we truly begin following Christ, or others can say it of us when they see how we have changed. And if you are still searching for that change, surrender everything to Christ (your life, your identity, to be solely bound up in His), follow His example, and watch Him work.

In Philippians 2:7, we saw how Christ humbled Himself simply by coming into the world as a human baby who would one day die. Yet now, on top of that, as a man, He humbled Himself again and became obedient unto death in the most torturous way. Christ was faithful to obey to the very end of His life on earth—an early end at that—but He obeyed anyway. When He grew weary, He prayed and still obeyed. Knowing how He would die, He requested the cup be taken away from Him, but He submitted to the will of God for the goodness of God to be shown (Luke 22:42).

Obedience is a sacrifice that God delights in. He said, "[This is] My beloved Son, in whom I am well pleased" (Mark 1:11). Does it make you glad when your children, or those you are responsible for, don't put obedience off? When I tell someone to do something and they drag their feet or put it off, that makes me feel like I do not matter to them and have no way of helping or making a difference in their lives. All I want at that moment is obedience. But when I see them doing what is right without being told, it makes my heart overflow with joy, and I want to shower them with gifts and words of affirmation and tell them "well done." Don't you think God, who knows all and especially what is best for everyone eternally, also feels what way? Don't you see that our obedience reflects our trust and faith in Him?

God does ask big things of His obedient servants. "Even the death of the cross," as our verse says. Being hung by your arms with nails in your extremities and having a crown of thorns pounded into your head after being severely whipped sounds like the most painful and humiliating way to die, yet Christ submitted to God and bore this death on the cross in order to obey the Father. Will we go that far to obey God? We must! If God calls us to it, we must. This is not to make life look bleak. It is a reminder: if we are not willing to live and die for Him, then our "to live" is not gain. Jesus said anyone who wanted to come after Him must "deny himself, and take up his cross daily, and follow Me" (Luke 9:23). If we don't and instead deny Him, His word says He will deny us (2 Timothy 2:12). Jesus warned that "difficult is the way which leads to life" (Matthew 7:14). But it is worth the pain. James and John's mother asked to have her two sons sit one at Christ's right hand and the other at His left. Jesus responded by asking them if they could drink the cup of suffering He was about to (Matthew 20:22). It is important that our mindsets be focused on God so that no matter what comes our way, what battles we face, or what trials arise, we stay true to Christ, even unto death. James would be the second martyr after Stephen. John would not face martyrdom—the only apostle to escape it—but he would face many other challenges in the name of Jesus. Even so, Jesus, out of submission to the Father, would not promise their seating arrangements in heaven. Our identity cannot be in position or hopes and dreams; it has to be in Christ alone. If your identity is focused on hopes and dreams, then when the trials, hardships, and battles of life come our way, we will crumble. But if our identity and hope are in Christ Jesus, we can stand, for the glory of God, and endure. All martyrs for Christ have had to hold on and remain steadfast in the Lord through traumatic experiences and horrific deaths. It is possible to hold on and obey, but we can only do that if the mind of Christ is in us. First Corinthians 13 says even if we are burned at the stake, but have not love, then we are nothing (1 Corinthians 13:1–13). The mind of Christ is one of love and obedience to the Father. We are to love the Lord with all our heart, soul, mind, and strength (Luke 10:27), and to do that, we hold nothing back; we surrender and obey no matter the cost. Jesus was completely obedient as a man, and the disciples were obedient unto death also. Are you in? In order to "be in," to endure in obedience, we have to be grounded in Christ and His Word. He makes us who we are. He is the reason why we do what we do. If He is not, we will flounder and not be able to stand in who we are when the hard times and persecution come. Find who you are in Christ by learning more about Him and standing in Him. Be obedient.

Application: Pray for obedience. Ask that your mind be transformed to one like Christ's that will obey no matter the cost and that your heart be focused on Him in the process.

How does obedience help us find our identity?

What does being "all in" with God look like in your life?

Describe a time when you experienced God changing you and you began stepping into your identity in Him?

If you have not experienced the change, seek out someone who has and ask them to share their testimony with you.

Day Fourteen

He Is Lord

Philippians 2:10–11

At the name of Jesus every knee should bow, of those in heaven, and of those on earth, and of those under the earth, and that every tongue should confess that Jesus Christ is Lord, to the glory of God the Father.

One semester, back in college, I was really struggling with my grades in this one online class. I refused to use an online source during the tests because it felt like cheating; the source seemed to have all the right answers for the tests. I studied hard, but I could not make sense of the class. I was doing what I believed was right and felt like I was being punished for it. At that time, my grades were kind of an idol for me. I found my identity in being an A student, so I was crushed when I received my first D. Not only was my grade struggling, but I was wrecked because being a good student was how I measured my worth. Grades, I thought, were the best thing going for me. I allowed my life to revolve around them. Since then I have matured in Christ and identify who I am in Him. I tell others that college is a season—that's it—and grades do not define who you are; Christ does. We are to give our best efforts but do so to please God not for the perfect score or to be validated in our accomplishments. We are to do everything to the glory of God (1 Corinthians 10:31). In His mercy, God did not allow me to find my worth in something that was not Him. As I was living for the grades, I thought it was proof that I was a good Christian, but that is not true. Sometimes I catch myself doing this at work, and I have to remind myself where my identity is found.

We can do this with anything that we are pouring ourselves into, and they are not in themselves bad things; in fact they are often good things: our studies, our work, our degrees, our accomplishments, our church, our role in the church, our families, our dreams, and so on. It was in a Bible study when God showed me that I was finding my identity in something other than Him. He opened my eyes and simply reminded me that He, not my grades, was Lord. I was to live for Him, not for them. I imagined that as I got to judgment and showed Him my grades they would burn up before Him because He wanted to know what I did for Him and not for my own achievements. An A in our academics means nothing in heaven; what God cares about is whether we are like His Son. Did we live and serve for the glory of God? This is why having the mind of Christ is so essential. This life is about glorifying God with all that we are. Every part of our lives must bow to the Father, the King of kings and Lord of lords, as Jesus did.

When a king enters, he is announced, and all people fall to their knees out of respect and reverence. Jesus is one with the Father and stands at His right hand. And scripture tells us that when He "comes in His glory . . . all the nations will be gathered before Him" (Matthew 25:31–32). At the name of Jesus, every knee will bow. Whether good or bad, every knee will bow. We don't have a choice on judgment day, and every tongue will, at the end, confess that Christ is Lord as our verse today says. Everyone, all of creation, the whole universe will admit to Christ being Lord. People may have lived a life of sin and shame or disbelief, but at the end, the entire world, whether they agree with Him or not, will confess that He is Lord. The Creator has declared it. All—the atheists, neotheists, Mormons, Buddhists,

Muslims, Hindus, and all other religions of this earth—will have to recognize and proclaim Christ as King and Lord. Blessed are those who do it now. We will certainly still bow and confess, but our end is heaven versus those who choose not to believe, whose end is hell. Each one of us has a choice on this earth to recognize Christ as Lord, but on judgment day the choice is gone. No more will people be blindly deceived, all will know the truth, and we will be judged according to what we did with it. On that day the whole world, past and present, will also see where every soul put their worth. Will it be in grades as I did, in what others think, sports, fame, money, family, friends, or some other noble cause, or will it be in Jesus Christ alone? If we put our love for anything above our love for Christ, then our "to die" is not gain. One pastor portrayed it as the dash between two dates on a tombstone. The dash represents our life, the dates are the beginning and the end. What we do with that dash, what we choose to believe and who or what we put our identity in, will determine our destination at the end of that last date. We can argue that truth is relevant, but at the end of the day the truth still exists, truth stands, and we will all be judged based on God's real truth.

When I was in college, God had to show me through my grades that, in the end, my grades will burn up before Him. What will remain is Christ in me, the works I did to obey and glorify Him, and my belief. Should I study hard? Yes, study to show yourself approved (2 Timothy 2:15) but not more so than obeying your Creator. Our foremost priority is to love and obey God; the second is to love and share Christ with others. One day truth will be revealed and the whole world will know it. Until then, it is our job to seek truth and preach it to those who are lost and perishing because they need to choose Christ, too, as what they are living for. It is a sad thought that all those who do not know Christ as their Lord will be constantly perishing. Yet there is hope for them as long as they are still living. Jesus gives us all another chance with each new day to choose Him, to choose His mindset, the eternal life He offers, with Him forever.

Application: Pray for a devoted heart and chances to express and confess that Christ is Lord of your life.

Christ being Lord of our life defines our identity how?

Are we like God's Son, Jesus?

What good things are we putting above God in our lives?

What are we going to do about it?

Are we working for our own glory or God's?

Day Fifteen

A Holy Fear

Philippians 2:12

Therefore, my beloved, as you have always obeyed, not as in my presence only, but now much more in my absence, work out your own salvation with fear and trembling.

A constant phrase in my home growing up was "Go put this up and then come right back." This is because as a small child, I could not be trusted to be productive on my own, and if I did not come right back, then I most likely would get into trouble of some sort. I was so easily distracted as a child. Besides, playing was so much more fun than cleaning. But Mom knew in her wisdom, in order to keep me out of trouble, I needed specific instructions to come right back. She explained that when my siblings and I were trustworthy, obeyed the first time and came back, and asked if there was anything else to help with, voluntarily, then she would know that we were being responsible. Our aim was to please Mom and do what was right. When we were responsible, she could leave us to work or play without parental supervision.

Children who lack maturity cannot be trusted to obey their parents. They have to constantly be maintained. These Christians in Philippi are young Christians, but they have matured and do the things they ought to without having to have Paul (their spiritual parent) around to remind them. However, they still need encouragement. They are kind of at the teenage point. In our home this was called the "adjustable" stage, which meant some days you were a child and some days you were a young adult. It adjusted based on your conduct and behavior. The Philippians knew what to do and they did it, but they were not independent and fully responsible yet. They were still learning who they were in Christ. Paul is desiring to help the Philippians grow to a level of maturity where their beliefs in Christ become their own. It is the change a child makes when they have not only adopted the beliefs of their parents but also taken ownership through searching the Scriptures, knowing and experiencing God themselves, and having a relationship with Him. We will not have our identity in Christ until we know Him. And our relationship with Christ is continuing to grow.

Hebrews encourages believers to move on from the milk of the word to the meat (Hebrews 5:12). Perhaps the Philippians were at vegetables, and Paul wants them to be spiritually ready for meat. So he tells them they are doing well, and now the next step is to work out their own salvation with fear and trembling. Paul means we are to search the word of God to understand our beliefs. It is a process of becoming our own person in Christ Jesus. This is scary, but it is the next step in becoming one with Christ, to make these beliefs our own. We already believe; now we are to draw near. To choose Him over our earthly desires. We do this through the power of God, a relationship with Jesus Christ, listening to the Holy Spirit, searching His word, and with wisdom from seasoned believers. This does not mean children do not ask their parents for wisdom and counsel, we should always ask our authorities, as we discussed earlier, but it is starting our own faith walk with Jesus to become who He wants us to be. It is making a covenant of our own and seeking His will for our lives.

Paul's desire is for the Philippians to stand strong with Christ in his absence. We have to know what we believe so that during the times of opposition, oppression, or persecution (which we are promised), we can stand with Christ. Our friends' faith, our parents' faith, or our spouse's faith will not stand for us. Their faith will help them stand, but when we are faced with trials and pain, it is our own relationship with Christ Jesus and the foundations of who we are in Him that will determine if we stand or fall. Sometimes we do not know what our response will be until it happens, but we prepare in the present to train ourselves to respond in accordance with the will of God in the future. We can do this by finding ourselves in Christ, choosing His mindset. Start seeing whom He sees us as, searching the Scriptures to find how He wants us to live, and how Christ chose to live. Similar to the Philippians, we must also stand strong in Christ even when our teachers are absent. Will we fail and mess up? Yes, but God in His mercy offers another chance if we will repent and try again.

"The fear of the LORD is the beginning of knowledge" (Proverbs 1:7). Here in America we don't fear the Lord anymore. We want Him as a big huggable friend who gives us good stuff and makes sure everything goes well for us. That is one part of God's plan, sure, especially eternally. Another and perhaps more accurate part is that His goal for us here is to make us into His own image, which calls for being tested through fire, enduring hardships, and overcoming trials and temptations. He does not just make our hardships go away because, if they did, we would not grow and bear fruit. We forget that He is the Creator and Judge. He can still make the ground open up and swallow people (Numbers 16:30). He still can strike with plagues, pestilence, and death, but He chooses to refrain. If we don't fear the Lord, then how do we work out our own salvation with fear and trembling? Also notice it is our own salvation, not someone else's.

No one else's salvation can save you, it has to be yours personally crafted by you and God. I will not go to heaven based on my parents' relationship and walk with God. They cannot save me. It is my individual walk with Christ. When I would get frustrated with my siblings getting away with things and me being caught, Mom would say, "You worry about you. Let me worry about them." Similarly, our salvation is something we must be constantly working on. God reveals more and more about Himself every time we read His word. It is our privilege to be able to constantly strive for holiness. This is what we call sanctification, the process by which we become more and more like Christ. We are the only ones who can be responsible for our understanding of what we believe. When we work out our own salvation (with fear and trembling), it strengthens our identity in Christ. Don't worry about what God has told others to do; you worry about what He has told you to do. In John 21, Peter has just been told the kind of death he will die for Christ, and Peter turns around and asks Jesus, "What about John?" Jesus tells Peter, "It does not matter, you follow Me" (John 21:20–22). I am so much like Peter, but I need to focus on obeying God first, learning to live with the mind of Christ. We do what is right in spite of everything going wrong because that is what Jesus has called us to do and what He expects us to do. It does not matter what others have as a mindset, you worry about yours.

Application: Ask the Lord to illuminate your path to understanding Him so that your beliefs may be founded on Him, the Rock of our salvation. Ask Him to help you make your beliefs your own.

How has your identity been shaped in your individual walk with God?

Is there someone you are allowing to carry your faith for you instead of making it your own?

How can you make your faith your own?

How does the fear of the Lord help us in our search for our identity?

Day Sixteen

With God

Philippians 2:13

For it is God who works in you both to will and to do for His good pleasure.

When we were young, Mom used to remind us that we were here to serve God. That is basically what Paul is saying here. She would ask, "Why were you born?" When I was little the answer was always, "To serve God." Since then, she has added to the answer and incorporated "To love God with all my heart, mind, and soul." If we do that, we will serve God. Our life here is not about us, it is about Him and what He has planned for us to do. Christ said that those who keep their lives will lose them, but those who lose them for Christ will gain them (John 12:25). We must lose ourselves, desires, wants, concerns so that we can find our identity in Christ. This "lose ourselves" does not mean go crazy, but it means to surrender, humble ourselves, to His will. Jesus said to seek first the kingdom of God, and all these things will be added (Matthew 6:33). As we learn to love God with all that we are, our views and desires, our mindset, will change to look more like His. We just have to seek Him and find what His desires and values are, and then be led by Him in every step, leaving Him room to redirect us.

Christ is our rock and our salvation (Psalm 62:2); we are His servants, and we should try to please Him. But the flesh is sinful and loud and demands its own way. Within ourselves and in our strength, we cannot please God (Romans 8:8). That is why it is God who works in us to will and do. We can't even breathe on our own; if He were to hold His breath, we would all die (Job 34:14–15). We, in ourselves, can do nothing. However, scripture tells me, "I can do all things through Christ who strengthens me" (Philippians 4:13). In the book of James, we are told, "Of His own will He brought us forth by the word of truth, that we might be a kind of firstfruits of His creatures" (James 1:18). He is like the garden working in our lives. The firstfruits are the beginning evidence of our identity; the firstfruits reveal who we are. In John 15:5, Jesus speaks of how we are branches that are to be inside Him gaining nutrients and life through Him, and without Him we can do nothing. It is God who works in us. However, we get to choose what kind of fruit we produce. A tree is known by its fruit (Matthew 12:33). We can desire to grow fruit for God, or we can harden our hearts and refuse. God works in our hearts and minds as we seek Him. However, when we do not seek Him, our hearts move in the opposite direction, and we become a tree no longer producing good fruit but bad. One example of this is with Pharaoh; he chose to harden his heart himself over and over again, refusing to let the people of Israel go free, and then God hardened his heart and cut him off, like a tree with bad fruit (Exodus 9:12). Another example is what God does in every new believer. When we search for God, He takes our heart of stone and replaces it with a heart of flesh (Ezekiel 36:26–27). He becomes our foundation, the basis of all the decisions of our heart. We see this in new believers all the time because they realize the gift God has given them, and they are "on fire" to do the will of our Savior no matter how big, no matter how small. They just want to serve Him right away. Proverbs says, "Commit your works to the LORD, and your thoughts will be established" (Proverbs 16:3). When we have our mind focused on Christ, we will bear good fruit.

As we seek God, we will find Him and we will fall more in love with Him, which makes us yearn to do His will. Our mindset changes from a sinner's to the mind of Christ. As we truly try to please Him, He will change our hearts to desire and want to do His good pleasure. We find our identity as we are transformed into the likeness of Christ. Another way I explain this is by using the illustration of a relationship. When we fall in love and are dating, our desires change. Our mindset begins to become similar to or line up with the person whom we love. We start dressing like they do, using the same phrases, making the same facial expressions. We start planning a future with that person. I have watched so many girls change to fit the guy they are dating, because it happens all the time. Some I have seen the girl changed for the better, some for the worse. Perhaps this is because they do not have their identity in Christ. Nevertheless, a person changing is so obvious in a relationship. It's the same with God. As we develop a relationship with Him and fall in love with Him, we will change for the better. Our wants will change to match His and to line up with Him. A relationship with Christ will always change us to become what is right and in alignment with the character of Christ. It is God who gives us those desires to change for the better because His thoughts are higher than our thoughts and His ways are higher than our ways (Isaiah 55:8–9). It is God who works in us both to will and to do His good pleasure. Are we seeking the will of God today? Wisdom says seek Him and you will find Him (Proverbs 8:17). The book of James tells us that all we have to do is ask in faith (James 1:5). Are we committing our works to the Lord, without complaining so that our thoughts can be established (Proverbs 16:3)? Are we asking for God to take us deeper in our relationship with Him so we can find our identity in Him? Where are we with God today?

Application: Ask God what His will is for you and pray for strength to accomplish it.

How is following Christ a part of our "identity" journey?

What does our relationship with Christ look like now?

How can we go deeper?

Day Seventeen

A Complaining Mind

Philippians 2:14

Do all things without complaining and disputing.

This was a common verse quoted in our home, especially when it was time to clean the kitchen or bathroom. (When there are ten kids in the house, there are a lot of dishes). Sadly, we too often allowed the complaining to be not just about the dishes, and we complained about people, things about ourselves we didn't like, or where God had us in life. One thing of mine I complained about was myself, but all that did was tear me down and give me a bad self-image. I had to remind myself that how I looked was not what defined who I am. My looks will change. My relationship with Christ, growing stronger and more beautiful in Him, is what defines who I am. Our life is full of "seasons"; some seasons we don't like. We have to have faith that God has us here for a reason and we must trust Him that He will shape us through this season of life. But we won't learn propriety if we are complaining. Also, when we complain about others, it creates disunity. When we were little, we often complained about our siblings. To help change our mindsets, Mom would make us say three things nice about them. It helped.

While this verse is pretty straightforward and a simple command, we often disregard it. Through this book of Philippians, Paul has encouraged unity and one mind, the mind of Christ. Complaining and arguing cause discord among the body of Christ, which produces the opposite effect of unity. "These things ought not to be so" (James 3:10). We are supposed to be united under God. The mindset of Christ is one of humility and obedience to the Father. Complaining and disputing have their foundations rooted in pride, which is the opposite of humility. "I'm right, you're wrong." "Why do I . . ." "This *always* happens to me." These are all centered around *I* and not Christ. When we complain, we are building an identity filled with doubt and anger. That is not who Christ wants us to be. Christ said He gives us His peace (John 14:27), but when we complain, we destroy peace and create disunity. It is alright to confront someone when things look unfair, but don't complain about it. There is a time to stand for your faith and for what is right, but mindless and meaningless arguments are wrong. We are to walk in one mind: the mindset of Christ. His sheep hear His voice and obey it because they have the mind to obey (John 10:27). He calls us to be holy as He is holy (1 Peter 1:16). It is not holy to be prideful and complain, creating disunity. Pride is the sin the devil committed because he didn't want Christ's mindset; he wanted to be God.

Because there are so many members in my family, people assumed we had lots of fights. After all, aren't siblings supposed to fight? I specifically remember one day in Sunday school when some ladies asked us if we fought and wanted to know how we handled conflict. However, we were not allowed to fight. Dad and Mom decided many years before I was born that there would not be fighting in our home. Now, we do have disagreements, but the key to a peaceful home is to not allow fighting in the soul. Stopping a fight starts in the heart, long before words and fists start flying. When life's challenges and problems arise, when there is strong disagreement, that is when we have to trust God to work through our authorities and keep our minds set on Christ.

Our minds need to be set on eternally valuable things because, as we read in verses 15 and 16 of Philippians 2, having the mind of Christ is to bring glory to God and be a light and a lamp to the world. The unity of Christ, both what He has with the Father and what He prayed for us to have as believers, will speak volumes (John 17). It is time for the church to unite under the mind of Christ, to stop arguing about nonsalvation issues, and to stop complaining in our personal lives. The fact that people from different backgrounds, cultures, social classes, jobs, opinions, political parties, and races can be united in one holy mindset is a force that will draw others to Christ and cannot be ignored.

Application: Pray and ask God to bring unity to the churches. Ask Him to begin to mold our minds and unite under His.

How does not having a complaining mind contribute to the formation of our identity?

Do you catch yourself complaining a lot or a little?

What are you complaining about?

What does God's word say about complaining?

How can we be less of a complainer?

What can we talk about instead of complaining?

Day Eighteen

The Mindset of Endurance

Philippians 2:16

Holding fast the word of life, so that I may rejoice in the day of Christ that I have not run in vain or labored in vain.

Solomon, who was known for his wisdom, said, "Buy the truth, and do not sell it" (Proverbs 23:23). In our society there has been a huge push for relative truth, which basically is changing the meaning of truth and making it ambiguous. It is saying that truth is whatever applies to you—however you want to interpret it—and whatever makes you feel justified or good about your person. In reality, truth does not change, and we must not give up the truth for fleeting fancies either. We ought not to let go of the eternal words of life, even when it is a hard word of communication and correction.

Jesus had just finished describing the significance of the Last Supper and predicting His death, when many of His followers left because His words were too hard to accept. But when asked if the twelve would leave, too, Peter said, "Where else would we go? No one else has the words of life" (John 6:60–71). Never give up the words of life; never let them go. Life with Jesus is too precious to surrender. Sometimes truth will cause us to question our identity, but we cannot be afraid of that. We should allow truth to mold and shape our identity in Christ, to allow Him to chip away at our identity when it is placed in anything but Him.

If we abandon the word of life, there is an eternal death that we will receive. Wide (easy) is the path that leads to destruction, and narrow (hard) is the path that leads to life (Matthew 7:13–14). Yes, it is an uphill climb to live as Christ, as Paul urges us, but better to be climbing upward away from hell below than to be sliding downhill fast on the way to eternal destruction and fire (Proverbs 15:24).

I have always been terrified of heights, but at the same time if there is a need, I want to be the one to help. So when a group of family and friends were building the house I mentioned earlier, there was this scaffolding that we used. It was very tall and made of platforms connected by pole-like ladders. I could climb to the second story. The third story, however, was terrifying because there were no side rails to hold on to, and I just could not do it. But I admired those who could. In life, God calls us to climb with Him. Sometimes it can be scary, but don't be like me, who just watched others climb. When it comes to God asking you to do something, hold on to the truth and climb despite the fear. He climbs with you. He will not leave you; be strong and of good courage (Deuteronomy 31:6).

Do we have the words of life and truth in our hearts, or have we given them up for fear, popularity, social agendas, to be normal or even for temporary peace? Yes, there will be times when we fall and let go of truth, but the Holy Spirit is there to pick us up if we will just grab hold.

> A righteous man may fall seven times
> And rise again,
> But the wicked shall fall by calamity. (Proverbs 24:16)

Do not let go of the true words of life, no matter how terrifying that may make you feel. God is working inside you.

Application: Ask Jesus to engrave the words of life on your heart. Thank Him for these words and ask for discernment to know the truth. Paul made it his mission when he was with the Corinthians to only know Christ and Him crucified (1 Corinthians 2:2). Christ is truth. He said, "I am the way, the truth, and the life. No one comes to the Father except through Me" (John 14:6).

How does pressing on, even when you are afraid, help find your identity in Christ?

How does endurance grow us in the mind of Christ?

What are some areas where we would be tempted to sell the truth?

How do we buy the truth and not sell it?

Week Three Overview

What did God teach you about your identity this week?

How can we help others find their identity?

How can people tell that Christ is Lord of your life?

What is the fear of the Lord?

How does humility grow our identity in Christ?

Day Nineteen

A Daily Choice

Philippians 2:17

Yes, and if I am being poured out as a drink offering on the sacrifice and service of your faith, I am glad and rejoice with you all.

Persecution is something we do not expect in extreme measures here in America. We can think that we will be like Paul and rejoice over being counted worthy to sacrifice and suffer for others, but until we are tested we will not know for certain. Now, there are steps to take in order to help prepare ourselves. For example, practicing self-control, showing kindness, thinking of others before ourselves, telling our desires (our flesh) no, waiting patiently in all things, taking thoughts captive and choosing to focus on God as Christ did, only getting what is needed at the store, being thankful and grateful, trying to find the positive, or looking for God in every situation would be some good steps to take. Mom tried to teach us this when we were little by telling us not to take the last cookie on the plate but to deny ourselves and offer it to the others first. When we scraped our knees, she would tell us to say "Praise God" to help us get our eyes and thoughts on God. Small things like that can be implemented to prepare for harder times. When choosing God and exercising self-control are an everyday response in our lives, it will become a natural response in all situations. Are we ready to start practicing?

Paul, in the book of Romans, tells us that we are to present our bodies as living sacrifices (Romans 12:1–2). Here he is living it out as he writes the letter to the Philippians while in prison. The drink offering was a daily offering made in the temple to the Lord (Exodus 29:38–42). Daily we are to die to our flesh (our earthly wants and desires); daily we are to put on the new man and choose not to put back on the old man; daily we must choose Christ. When we do this we are being renewed and formed "according to the image of Him who created [us]" (Colossians 3:9–10). Furthermore, putting God before our will and desires, offering Him all that we are and submitting to His will constantly is part of our gift to Christ. This is a sacrifice pleasing to God. What David tells us is a contrite and broken spirit is an offering God will not reject (Psalm 51:17). When we humble ourselves and submit to the will of God, then He can use us to our full potential. That is when we bloom in who we truly are when we step fully into our identity as children of God. Often it is not until we give up ourselves to God that we see God work in miraculous ways.

When I was young and in college, I gave my desire of getting married to God; it was then that He taught me what it was like to love and have joy in Him. He took what He was teaching me and turned it into my first book: *First and Forever: Singleness in Ephesians*. He waited to teach me until I was ready to sacrifice all my hopes and dreams for Him. Now staying in that mindset is a continual decision I must make. Sacrifices are rarely pleasant, but they get us to a point of recognizing who God is and to a point of submission. James says, "Submit to God. Resist the devil and he will flee from you. Draw near to God and He will draw near to you" (James 4:7–8). Jesus and His disciples sacrificed everything for the glory of God. What are we truly willing to give up for God?

Application: Ask God to fill you with Himself so that you may be satisfied in Him and know that He is enough.

How can daily dying to self create your identity in Christ?

What habits can you begin to help form your identity and have a mindset like Christ?

When we practice making our daily decision about Christ, what does it teach us based on ourselves?

Day Twenty

Rejoicing in Affliction

Philippians 2:18

For the same reason you also be glad and rejoice with me.

I have a friend who was your normal outdoorsy girl who loved all things country. One day she came down with a life-altering condition. For years her life would be filled with doctors, procedures, hospitals, nurses, insurance issues, and research. By the time we met, she was in a wheelchair but smiling, friendly, and full of wisdom in the word of God. Some of us might ask where is the good in this? She is amazing and has so much to offer the world, but often we ask this because we do not know God as we should and don't know the vessel of circumstances He chooses to use. This individual carries joy with her all the time. She is the picture of endurance and determination. She works through the pain and tries to walk as much as she can without a wheelchair. She learned to find her identity in Christ and not her life dreams of the past, not the diagnosis, and not her circumstances. When we look for the "good," we are often looking for physical things, but what about spiritual things? Her enduring through suffering built character. In the book of Romans, Paul tells the church that we are to glorify God in tribulations and trials, and it will produce perseverance, character, and hope (Romans 5:3–4). So what good could come out of this? So much more than we realize. She is an example to all those around her of endurance through suffering with joy and faith. In our Bible study, she is a constant reminder for us to keep pressing on, to keep having faith in God, and to keep loving God when hard times completely change our lives. She could have lost her identity to the condition of her body, but instead she has allowed her trials to firmly root her into who she is in Christ. So, we thank God for this wonderful friend and the example she is to me and all who really get to know her.

Paul asks the Philippians to rejoice in his suffering with him because of the fruit it will bring about. James tells us to "count it all joy when you fall into various trials, knowing that the testing of your faith produces patience. But let patience have its perfect work, that you may be perfect and complete, lacking nothing" (James 1:2–4). Both Paul and James are calling believers to rejoice in trials and hardships for the fruit that will come. But fruit will only come if we allow God to work in us and if we embrace what He wills to teach us. This is a different mindset than what most of us have. However, if we look, Paul and James are both grateful for the spiritual growth taking place during hard times. This is the key. It is getting our minds off the present circumstances and onto God to see how He will grow, shape, and mold us. Hebrews tells us in hard times to look to Jesus, "the author and finisher of our faith, who for the joy that was set before Him endured the cross" (Hebrews 12:2). The joy set before us in hard times is that we are being refined and our spirit is being made to be more like Jesus. He wants us to be holy, as He is holy (1 Peter 1:16). Trials and hardships, just like showers, scrub away the gunk and clean our being. If we cleave to Jesus, He will bring us through.

God is never far from us (Matthew 28:20). We are never alone in a trial; Jesus promised, "I will never leave you nor forsake you" (Hebrews 13:5). My friend in the wheelchair is not alone in her trials; she has God, and in His mercy He sent her to me and our group of friends. She could have given up and resigned herself to her condition and to feelings of loneliness, but she did not; she kept pressing into God and being available to Him leading her. Fix your eyes upon Jesus. Don't be like Peter, who took his eyes off Christ and turned to watch the waves of this world beating him down. When he did, he began to sink, and so will we (Matthew 14:28–32). If we look at the circumstances and not to the One who controls the circumstances (and who knows the outcome), we will not last long before we sink like Peter. Call out to God. Refocus. Trust Him in the hard times; rejoice and be glad. Blessed are those whose eyes are stayed on Christ (Isaiah 26:3).

Application: Ask the Lord to help us see the good in our trials so that we may rejoice in them as we are directed to.

How can we, like my friend, find our identity in Christ in spite of the challenges of life?

Are we letting a condition or circumstance define us or become our identity?

How does endurance impact us or what role does endurance play in our lives?

Where has God used your trials for good?

Day Twenty-One

Humility and Growth

Philippians 2:22

But you know his proven character, that as a son with his father he served with me in the gospel.

When I was in high school, I competed at the national level for a speech competition. At this competition we gave an eight-to-ten-minute speech on the United States Constitution and then a second shorter speech on one of five pulled topics from a portion of the Constitution. When I made it to the national level, I represented my entire state. I may have been the only Alabamian those other competitors will ever meet, so however I acted would impact their opinion of my state. Furthermore, when I got home, I was the one who got to represent and tell about the competition to other competitors and prep them for when they might get to go.

Paul is getting ready to send Timothy to the Philippians so that Timothy may report back to Paul how the church in Philippi is doing (Philippians 2:19). Timothy is going as an ambassador for Paul, to do a wellness check. He also represents Paul to his church. We, too, as Christians, are like representatives. Now we can get caught up in self-importance and all puffed up with ourselves; we fall into the trap of building our identity based on others' views and the perceived importance of our roles. But when we do this, we get in the way of God using us. God resists the proud according to the Bible, but He honors the humble (James

4:6, 10 and Matthew 23:12). Timothy chose to be humble and reliable, truthful and faithful, which is why Paul chose him.

Timothy is an example of humility and growth. Humility because he is ready to serve Paul in any capacity. We can see growth of his humility from earlier in his life when he listened to and was taught by his mother and grandmother, and now God has promoted him to learn under Paul (2 Timothy 1:5). He begins as a son to Paul and a messenger to go and see how the churches are doing. He is faithful in that job and is eventually given the responsibility of the church in Ephesus to be their preacher and leader (1 Timothy 1:2–20). Timothy was humble and faithful with little yet important things, and then was entrusted with greater things. In Jesus's teaching, He told of good and faithful servants who, because they were faithful over few things, were entrusted with more (Matthew 25:21–23). Paul also is exhorting Timothy's character in the above verse, perhaps to point him out as a role model or to esteem him to the Philippians so that they would welcome him. Timothy is defined here as a son with a proven character. He has been trusted, tried, and found to be exactly as he should be.

Can people say that about us? Or do we fall into the category of hypocrite, where we are one way at church and another in the grocery store? Are we the ones who push people away from Jesus because we have a character of being two-faced? Sometimes when tested, we really get to see how much of a hypocrite we are. Through the years I have been tested many times. As I observed myself, I was shown the hypocritical flaws that God was trying to purge me from. His desire is for me to be found just as I should be, faithfully pursuing Him as Timothy did. During a national crisis, I was not having the mind of Christ, and I became angry at so many things while God was trying to teach me to trust Him. It's easy to say we trust God, but when the rubber meets the road, we will find out if we are hypocrites or not. The good news is, even if we find ourselves to be hypocrites, Christ can help us regain that mind of Christ and change. In Psalm 139, David prayed,

> Search me, O God, and know my heart;
> Try me, and know my anxieties;
> . . . .
> And lead me in the way everlasting. (Psalm 139:23–24)

When He lives within us, and we allow Him to take up residence in every part of us, we will change as a result. As we have a relationship with God, He will mold us and transform us to the image of His Son, He will instill in us the heart of a servant. That is what Timothy allowed God to do in him. Let us also allow ourselves to be transformed through Christ Jesus.

Application: Pray as David did and ask the Lord to test you and show you where you sin and need to improve so that you will be found as Timothy was, exactly as you should be.

How does being like Timothy grow our identity?

What are the areas of pride in our lives that we need to be careful of?

Who is one godly role model whom you want to learn from as Timothy did with Paul?

How can we grow our humility and faithfulness?

Day Twenty-Two

Mercy of God

Philippians 2:27

For indeed he was sick almost unto death; but God had mercy on him, and not only on him but on me also, lest I should have sorrow upon sorrow.

Recently, God asked me for a sacrifice of a relationship with someone whom I had become very fond of. This was very difficult, but God in His mercy gave me the strength to obey. The road of trusting God with this sacrifice is not easy and is not over. There are still very hard days. However, every day when it is hard, God reminds me that He has got me and this situation is in His hands. That is the mercy and grace of God to walk this path with me, confirming His will and giving me strength and assurance through His tender whispers. In addition, walking through this trial has allowed me the opportunity to encourage others, not that God will fix the situation according to our standards but that God is good and faithful through it. After all, our faith is in God's love and goodness, not in getting what we want. When we have walked with God through something hard like that, it teaches us how far God is willing to walk with us. We also learn how far we will go and how much we will give up for God. And over all, it takes us deeper into our relationship with Christ. When we have gone deeper with Christ, we gain confidence in our identity in Him and can teach others as they walk through valleys too.

Paul takes this moment to remind the church (through the healing of Epaphroditus) that God is merciful and answers prayers. The Love of God endures forever and His mercy to all generations (Psalm 100:5). Our God is active, moving, and alive! He constantly intervenes in our lives. In Luke, it is recorded that Jesus told Peter, "I have prayed for you" (Luke 22:31–34). Romans tells us that the Holy Spirit makes intersession on our behalf when we don't know what to pray (Romans 8:26–27). I don't know how many times I have held onto this verse as I have walked through heart-wrenching pain and not knowing what to pray. When that happens, I say, "Holy Spirit, You know what to pray, so please intercede on my behalf," and He does. God still heals and still moves today, but even if He chooses not to He is always with us. "I will never leave you nor forsake you," He says (Joshua 1:5 and Hebrews 13:5). Paul reminds believers of this not only by pointing out that God healed his friend but also by magnifying God's mercy.

When I walked through the trial of sacrificing my relationship to God, I was constantly reminding myself of the mercies and goodness I had seen God do. That was essential to my endurance and strengthened my identity deeper in Christ. It is important that we remember God's mercy; it is a truth that will strengthen us in the hard times. We fix our eyes on Christ, the Author and Finisher of our Faith (Hebrews 12:1–3). He will give us strength. Christ embodied God's mercy to us when He humbled Himself taking on the form of a bondservant and coming in the likeness of men to die on the cross for each one of us (Philippians 2:5–8). I believe we will find God's mercy if we look for it. A few years ago, I started keeping up with a list of things I am grateful for. I would add to it every night to train myself to look for and remember the mercies of God. Sometimes it may simply be the fact that He is near and not letting us go through pain and suffering alone. Whatever it may be, when we praise God, our praise transforms our minds to be more like Christ. One way I learned God's mercy was by watching some friends continue to show love and mercy to someone who was constantly bringing them pain. They have given years of repeated mercy for repeated offenses. Often, I have thought to myself, if these friends, who are human, can extend that much mercy, then God's mercy, which is far beyond theirs, is phenomenal. Because of His mercy, in the hard times, all we have to do is reach out and touch Him like the woman who had the issue of blood, and He will get us through victoriously, instilling in us the mind of Christ (Luke 8:43–48). Will you reach out to Him in your struggles and allow yourselves to lean on Christ through them?

Application: Take some time thanking God for His unending mercies. Praise Him for them and ask that He open your eyes to recognize His mercy everywhere.

How does seeing the mercies of God shape our identity?

Name ten mercies of God you have seen in the last week.

Where have you seen the mercies of God in your own past trials?

Day Twenty-Three

A Servant's Heart

Philippians 2:29–30

Receive him therefore in the Lord with all gladness, and hold such men in esteem; because for the work of Christ he came close to death, not regarding his life, to supply what was lacking in your service toward me.

There is a man at church who gives of his time, money, ability, and hard work. If he knows there is need for a woodworking project, he is there to fix it or make it happen. When the church needed remodeling, he was the main driving force; he had the vision, the plan, the cool tools, and the organization to complete it. Both the man Paul is talking about and this man at our church are servants. Another dear couple I know are always in the background serving here and there. Often you will find them in the kitchen helping serve food to young adults who come to our church or building ramps for the disabled. They put the needs of others first. Look for servants, because they shine with the servant heart of our Savior.

These men and women, who give all of themselves to Christ and His work, are to be esteemed, noted, and set as an example to learn from. In our current lives we esteem movie stars, rich and famous people, or historical figures, but Paul encourages us to respect the meek, lowly, servants, and humble individuals. The man who came, in order to bring encouragement to Paul, came despite the health challenges and the consequences. He had the mind of Christ, a servant to those in need no matter the cost. When our identity is in Christ, we learn to look out for others more than ourselves, as Christ did also.

Jesus, the Messiah and God, took on the form of not only a bondservant to become like us but also the lowliest servant when He washed the disciples' feet (John 13:2–5). Christ encouraged them and us to do the same. It was not socially correct for Jesus, their teacher, to wash the disciples' feet, yet He did it, and He tells us to do the same. When Dad was teaching a Sunday night class about how a Christian family should look, he washed mom's feet in front of everyone and then encouraged all the men to do the same. I don't fully know what it is, but this gesture of servitude always blesses the wives. Just as it blesses the ladies, it blesses God when we serve others in His name by physically washing their feet or by serving them in other ways. As we children had all grown up into adulthood and were moving our separate ways about the country, Mom took an opportunity to teach us all one last lesson. She called a family meeting and had each of her children take their shoes off and put their feet into a warm basin of water. Her lesson was that if she, as Mom, would serve us, we should always serve one another no matter where life takes us. Then of course, my little sister put it right into practice and washed Mom's feet.

It will not be socially acceptable for us to do some things God may call us to, but it will be right. Whom do you want to be identified with? Society or God? Society does not define us. Our Creator does because He knows the person He designed us to be before we were ever thought of by our parents. Which is more important to us: to be correct and in good standing with society or to be righteous and in right standing with God? Sadly, sometimes we choose society over Christ, but we must practice choosing Christ. To live is Christ and to die is gain (Philippians 1:21). As proclaimed Christians we ought to live as Christ did, bringing glory to God. This friend of Paul's gave his all, which nearly included giving his own life to serve God and His people. What will we give up for Christ? Friends, relationships, wealth, fame, a future? If we are to live with Christ's mindset we must ask ourselves what we hold higher than obeying God. Or ask, is obeying God our top priority? Do we act like it?

Application: Ask God for the grace to hold nothing back from Him and nothing back from obeying and serving Him. Pray that we get to the point in our relationship with Him where we will obey without hesitation.

How does being a servant define your identity?

Whom do you want to be identified with?

Where can you serve God in your life?

Who in your sphere of friends are servants and how can you tell?

Day Twenty-Four

Always Do What Is Right

Philippians 3:1

Finally, my brethren, rejoice in the Lord. For me to write the same things to you is not tedious, but for you it is safe.

One saying my mom used to always tell me was, "You worry about you." This was typically a response to me complaining about how a sibling was not corrected or punished and I was and how it was not fair according to my sense of justice. My childish heart called for immediate justice to be done and for them to get the same punishment I received or would have had I committed the same offense. Honestly, Mom probably did punish them, or just had not gotten around to it yet, but that was not fast enough for my little heart. She also used to tell me to pick my battles, because I wanted to fight for everything I believed in or something that I thought needed to be fixed. The saying "You worry about you" teaches that we are supposed to do good, worry about how we are responding, and leave the consequences of others' actions to God and those in authority. We are always to do what is right before God and let Him take care of all the other injustices.

Do not grow weary of doing good, for in the end when you have endured, you will receive a crown of life (Galatians 6:9). Throughout his letters, Paul constantly encourages the churches to endure and do what is right, always. The Philippians accepted Paul's words even though they had heard them before from Paul. They did not grow weary of his encouraging instructions to rejoice in the Lord even though they had seen pain and loss in their fellow Christians' suffering. Those who love and receive instruction will be wise, Proverbs informs us (Proverbs 19:20). To grow and mature in our identity in Christ, we must be humble and willing to listen to instruction and endure. Paul is encouraging the church to continue to do well and have the mind of Christ, who lived the ultimate example of rejoicing in trials. When we have the mindset of Christ, our whole perspective changes. We will no longer be conformed to this world but will be transformed by the renewing of our minds (Romans 12:2). If we put God's word and thoughts in place of our own, we start focusing on how we obey God instead of the injustices of our pains. We no longer need affirmation from the world but instead look to the Author and Finisher of our faith to know our identity and our worth. Our mindset astronomically affects how we react to our circumstances. This is why we need to cultivate the mind of Christ within ourselves, so we will respond in a manner that glorifies the Father and is in alignment with our identity in Christ Jesus.

Our Lord constantly spent time with the Father. When we pray, it is a time of private intimacy where we pour our hearts out to God. So when you pray, go into your room and pray to your Father in secret who hears in secret (Matthew 6:5–6). Jesus is our example. He was alone in the wilderness; He went alone to be with God when the five thousand followed Him and after He fed them. Feeding the five thousand, by the way, was right after Jesus's cousin, John the Baptist, was executed. Realize that at a very difficult personal time in Jesus's earthly life, He went to get alone with God, but when God sent Him people to serve, He performed one of the largest miracles ever! He also went alone into the garden of Gethsemane to pray before His crucifixion (Matthew 14:22–23; Luke 4:1–2; 22:40–42).

Having the mind of Christ is an everyday process, which is why Paul writes to remind them, "To live is Christ, and to die is gain" (Philippians 1:21). This is so contrary to our way of thinking that it is often tough to understand, much less to live out. But the mind of Christ is not the easy way. Wide (easy) is the gate that leads to destruction, but narrow (challenging) is the gate that leads to life (Matthew 7:13). Whenever I was struggling to keep my mind focused on God, as it seemed those who abandoned the narrow path were receiving all the "blessings" and I was not, God gently reminded me that I am to do what is right in spite of everything going wrong because Jesus expects and calls me to live righteously. That is one of the reminders I have taped to my desk at my office. The path of having the mind of Christ is not easy, but we rejoice because His path leads to life.

Application: Pray and ask God for endurance and His strength. We all need water to live, and we will grow weary, but when we do, we must go to the One who can revive us.

How does always doing what is right affect our identity?

Where do you need to practice "you just worry about you" and not what God is doing in other people's lives?

Share about a time when you were weary and God called you to do something.

How can we cultivate the mind of Christ in these situations?

Week Four Overview

What did God teach you about your identity this week?

What is a daily choice you are going to be intentional about making to help keep the mind of Christ?

How have you seen your identity in Christ grow?

What are you going to do to keep the mercies of God at the forefront of your mind?

Day Twenty-Five

A Circumcised Heart

Philippians 3:3

For we are the circumcision, who worship God in the Spirit, rejoice in Christ Jesus, and have no confidence in the flesh.

Circumcision was a covenant among Abraham, his descendants, and God that set them apart (Genesis 17:10–12). It involved removing a boy's foreskin. This may not seem to affect women, but Christ desires us to be circumcised in the hidden parts of our heart, allowing things that do not line up with our identity in Him to be cut off from us. God was circumcising my heart when He asked me to say goodbye to a relationship I wanted so strongly. The relationship did not align with whom God has called me to be, even though I wanted it and would have changed to keep it. God asked me to allow Him to cut it off. Did it hurt? You bet it did. But that is what we call purification. The process of purification is where we get to choose. Will we say something God wants is too hard and change our identity so we become aligned with something other than Him? Or will we allow our identity to be built and centered on Christ Jesus? As we allow God to cut off, circumcise, that which He chooses, He is fashioning and setting our identity. Likewise, who we are in Christ will be defined by our allowance of God to cut away what He sees as excess. He circumcised my heart in many ways. Not only was the relationship "cut off," but God also used this to teach my heart the importance of cleaving to Him alone. He cut off the excess parts that were competing for my heart. God's circumcision is painful, yet it is physically and spiritually healthy for the whole body. The good news is He who circumcises us heals us. He says, "I wound and I heal" (Deuteronomy 32:39).

God's children will show the signs of circumcision in our hearts and lives, not necessarily physically but characteristically. When Stephen spoke to the Pharisees and called them uncircumcised, it was a full-blown insult, but he was meaning in their hearts (Acts 7:51). They had not set their hearts apart from this world. They were not allowing God to strip away the things that competed for His place in their hearts. They were still so consumed by the power in this world that they could not see the truth Christ brought.

Christ in us brings everything to the next level. Same with circumcision, it was no longer about the body but about cutting off the excess fleshly desires of the heart spiritually. The early believers quarreled over this because the Jews wanted to force the gentiles to follow their earthly circumcision laws, but the disciples and Paul knew it was about the heart. How many of us have excess flesh around our hearts and lives that we have not allowed God to remove yet? By excess flesh, I mean sins, iniquities, or anything that covers our heart so that Jesus cannot touch that section of who we are. Jeremiah says, "Circumcise yourselves to the Lord, and take away the foreskins of your hearts" (Jeremiah 4:4). Yet we constantly cover our hearts. We cling to things of this world when Christ desires us to cling to Him (Deuteronomy 30:20). Honestly, excess in anything, whether bad or good, that blocks Jesus from being able to touch our hearts and transform them into the identity He has for us is bad. It stops us from becoming the women of God He designed us to be before we were born. He desires our whole heart, not just sections of it.

One day, as I walked out of the house to go to work, Mom shouted after me, "Remember why you were born." This is a common phrase in our home to remember why God created us and to keep our focus on Him. So I began to recite the familiar passage beginning with "Love the Lord your God with all . . ." and I stopped there because He convicted me that there was something blocking my all from Him. He wanted my all, and I was not loving Him with all. Sure I loved Him, but with everything? Again, He took it to the next step for me. As Christians, we are supposed to die to the flesh and all its fleshly desires, basically anything that does not bring God glory and anything He decides does not match with the identity design He has for us. That means to get rid of the old man and his old identity and put on the new man and the new identity in Christ (Ephesians 4:24). It means to die to self, to take up our cross daily and follow Christ (Matthew 16:24). I am not there yet, and every time a portion of my flesh has to die, I fight it. I do not want to give it up, but if God has asked it, I ought to trust His master plan.

What I should be doing is surrendering because I should want God's will more than mine since I know it is for my good. It is His best for me. After humbling myself and obeying, I can always look back and see how my flesh being cut off was best for me, but in the moment, it is hard to kill the fleshly desires. Christ, in His mercy, is patient with me. His love for us is greater, better than our love for ourselves; therefore, our hearts are to be renewed and transformed to the will of God (Romans 12:2). How can we completely do that if there is flesh around our hearts, closing them off from God? First, don't fight what God has asked us to cut off. Second, trust Him and allow your identity in Him to be solidified. We are not supposed to stay the same but constantly be transformed to be more and more like Christ. "Be holy, for I am holy," Christ said (1 Peter 1:16). Next, we must fight with our flesh and resist temptations; God has provided a way out. Sometimes the way out is uncomfortable, cramped, and painful, but we must want God's will above ours so much that we are willing to take the way of escape offered to flee from where God does not want us. Finally, have no confidence in the flesh but be circumcised in your heart and serve God.

Application: Ask the Lord, as David did, to examine your heart and to remove the excess flesh so that your heart may be all His.

How does a circumcised heart form our identity?

Have you allowed God to remove the excess in your life?

If not, how will you surrender this to Him? Name the area that does not need to have a place in your heart and surrender it to the Lord, allowing God to circumcise it.

Day Twenty-Six

The Churchy Checklist

Philippians 3:5

[I was] circumcised the eighth day, of the stock of Israel, of the tribe of Benjamin, a Hebrew of the Hebrews; concerning the law, a Pharisee.

Way back in college, my friend and I were driving to Florida for a conference, and she asked me what God was teaching me. During that time, He was teaching me humility. She was shocked at my answer, but this is something God chooses to work on with me regularly. I believe that those of us who were raised in the church have to be vigilant to stay humble because we have the truth. We have not known a life without truth and that can make us even more susceptible to the sin of pride. We know all the right answers and how to make religion and hypocrisy look good. And that is what God was working on with me. He did not want me to just know the right answers; He wanted me to know Him. As we continue to see, Christ was humble, and if I want to know Him and identify with Him, then I, too, will work on humility. God can use us best when we are humble.

If the Pharisees had a checklist of everything that it took to be a good Jew and to walk holy before God, Paul was the role model follower. He had all the credentials but not the relationship before his encounter with Jesus. Paul had part of the truth but not all. Christ was not a part of his life at that time. In his letter, he is describing himself before his transformation from a persecutor to a follower. He speaks of how nothing compares to the knowledge of knowing Jesus Christ (Philippians 3:8). Meeting a religious checklist does not matter. What matters is, Are we following God's heart? Are we one with Christ? Do we have the mind of Christ? Do we meet His standards? One time, I was pouring my life into good church projects, and really, I was using that to keep busy and run away from the pain of rejection I was going through. During this time, I was challenged to "be still, and know that [He is] God" (Psalm 46:10). Everything I was doing went on pause for a month as God and I spent time together practicing being still before Him. I unknowingly needed that to take my relationship with Christ deeper because I was about to go through some very difficult things. I did not realize it at the time, but God used pausing good church things to spiritually strengthen and prepare me for what was coming. Had my identity been wrapped up in the outwardly busy things I was doing and not in Christ, as He helped me to do by being still, I do not know how well I would have done in the struggles that came.

We don't want to just pass the "church" checklist; we want to be striving for commendation and approval from God (1 Corinthians 10:18). All of these qualifications Paul counts as nothing compared to the joy of knowing Christ (Philippians 3:7–11). Nothing else compares and nothing else can get us to where we need to be. Jesus is "the way, the truth, and the life. No one comes to the Father except through [Him]" (John 14:6). We can spend our whole lives in a church, but if we don't have a relationship with Christ, He will say, "I never knew you" (Matthew 7:23). We can be as lost as a ball in high weeds while in church, because the right answers are not going to get us to God; Christ and only Christ is! All of these good works and church checklists should follow a born-again person and be evidence of our relationship with Christ, but they do not save us. The Bible does tell us that faith without works is dead (James 2:14–26). So the things we do should show our devotion to Jesus, but our identity should not be wrapped up in them because God may tell us to let go, or hold still, and then what? Will we say no or will we obey because who we are is based on Christ and not our church activities? We should have good works because they are evidence of our faith, but more important we must have a relationship with Jesus Christ. There is not a cookie cutter for the Christian life because we each were created uniquely and serve a different purpose, but our core is the same: following Christ. For this we need a relationship with Him and the mind of Christ, who was obedient unto death (Philippians 2:5–8). A relationship with Christ that exceeds death is what we are after. Please understand, I greatly support and encourage attending church and doing church activities, but the point is not to get so involved in them that your identity is being found in church activities and not Christ. The activities will not save us, Christ will. Be in church, yes. Lead and participate in Bible studies, encourage one another, teach a class, do what God has asked you to do for His kingdom, but keep it in focus where we do not lose who we are doing it for.

Application: Ask Christ to show you His list of standards so you don't get caught in the trap of meeting the "churchy" checklist. Now we need to pray for strength, because when God shows us His list, it can be overwhelming, but He helps us and expects us to obey.

How does avoiding the churchy checklist impact our identity?

Are you keeping up with a churchy checklist or is the basis of what you do based on Christ?

Examine your activities and your heart. Is what you are doing based on the "church" checklist or on a relationship you have with Christ?

Day Twenty-Seven

He Is Worth the Cost

Philippians 3:8

Yet indeed I also count all things loss for the excellence of the knowledge of Christ Jesus my Lord, for whom I have suffered the loss of all things, and count them as rubbish, that I may gain Christ.

As I processed saying goodbye to a romantic relationship, I was feeling punished by God. It looked like those around me were about to get what they wanted—a reward to my mindset—but I was left aching with nothing. During this time, I had to fight for my hope in God, to remind myself that I had lost nothing because I said goodbye in obedience to Him in comparison to what Christ had chosen to sacrifice for me. There is no sacrifice too great for God. It is challenging to keep this mindset, but even Jesus endured the cross for the eternal joy set before Him (Hebrews 12:2). Everything in this world is worthless compared to Jesus Christ in the eternal scheme of things. It is a constant struggle in this world of temptations to keep this view, so we continuously choose to align ourselves with, identify ourselves with, and trust Jesus. On the other side of that breakup, as miserable as it was, I can look back and see where God has established my identity in Him because of my obedience in letting go, trusting Him in His path for my life.

Paul, who was perfect according to the Pharisee law, counts everything here in this life as loss compared to knowing Jesus. He did not hold on to worldly things, status or fame, or even the religious "churchy" checklist. He learned these things do not get us where we need to be with Christ and God. In fact, sometimes they hold us back from reaching our potential. If we are focused on pleasing men before God, our life will be wasted. They are not our judge at the end; God is.

When Peter and John taught the people early in their ministry, they were arrested and brought before the Jewish elders. When told to stop preaching about Jesus, the apostles replied, "We ought to obey God rather than men" (Acts 5:29). They knew whom they would stand before and give an account to at the end of their lives—and it was not the Pharisees; it was God. They had left everything for Jesus, and they would not stop following Him now. When we honor God above all others, when we love Him more than anything else, we are following the greatest commandment: "Love the LORD your God with all your heart" (Matthew 22:32–38). It is harder for a rich man to enter heaven than for a camel to go through the eye of a needle (Matthew 19:24). We are to place our identity in God and nothing else. The disciples left their boats, their livelihoods, their heritage, and followed Christ (Luke 18:28). The rich young ruler was told that the one thing he lacked was to sell all he had, give to the poor, and follow Christ (Mark 10:17–31). From a worldly mindset, it is hard to understand and difficult to count everything as loss, but at the end of our life it is all dust and all temporary. People's opinions—temporary. Wealth—temporary. Health—temporary. Beauty—temporary. Popularity—temporary. And everything we love that is of the earth—temporary. God is eternal, and He wants our soul, which is also eternal.

In the book of Luke, Jesus taught that unless you hate your family you are not fit to be a disciple (Luke 14:26). To me, that means my family cannot rank above Christ on my love thermometer. A love thermometer is a visual way to see where the things in my life fall in respect to one another, and ultimately where Christ is in the lineup of all that. Christ wants our whole heart and soul. He allows us to have room for our family, but no greater relationship on this earth or beyond will exist like the one between us and Christ. This will be our clear choice, so much that nothing else will even appear on our love thermometer. We are placed on this earth to serve and glorify God. We do this by loving Him with our heart, mind, and soul. This life is a training ground preparing us for eternal life with Christ in glory. Everything else is simply a tool to teach us about the love of God and how to love God by identifying ourselves with His Son.

Application: Pray for understanding of the vast importance of your and Christ's relationship. Ask the Holy Spirit to grow that relationship in you.

How does the fact that Christ is enough shape our identity?

What has been something you were asked to give up by God?

What is something good that has come from this trial?

Day Twenty-Eight

Suffering

Philippians 3:10

That I may know Him and the power of His resurrection, and the fellowship of His sufferings, being conformed to His death.

There was an old widow I had known since I was a toddler. She never had much to live on but was always content. Throughout her life she endured great suffering through the early death of a child and then in her old age she endured injustice after injustice from relatives. I wanted to shake them and force them to treat this saintly woman with the love and care she deserved, but it was not my place. Although they took advantage of her and did not treat her well, she never complained. In her attempt to live with the mind of Christ, she would just keep turning the other cheek because she did not want to give any cause for those relatives to complain about Jesus. One day she even apologized for correcting one of them because she was concerned that it was too harsh. Her choice was to endure suffering instead and be as docile as a lamb, as our Savior was in His suffering. Even though she has now passed, she has left behind a legacy of one willing to endure anything for the good name of Christ. She did not identify with her circumstances, did not wallow in her misfortunes, did not complain nor fight for her "rights," but instead she identified with Christ in suffering.

Paul's mention of resurrection, suffering, and death is describing his relationship with Christ and his desire to be conformed to the likeness of Christ. Back in verse 8 he was saying how nothing compares to knowing Christ Jesus. Here he desires to be one with Christ. This is the mysterious oneness that is between a husband and a wife (which Paul describes in Ephesians 5:31–32), an intimate knowledge and relationship. It is not enough for Paul just to know about Jesus, but he wants to experience life with Him in the good times and in the struggles. Paul absolutely wants to be where Jesus is. He wants to be identified with Christ. Our relationship with Christ is supposed to be the love beyond death that a husband and a wife desire (Ephesians 5:23–33). A man and woman joined together in marriage somehow spiritually become one flesh (Mark 10:8). They sacrifice for each other and put the needs of the other above their own. Their souls become similar as they grow and abide together. Christ, when praying in the garden before He died, prayed that we would be one in Him (John 17:21).

Paul desires to know the power of Christ's resurrection and to partake in His suffering. No one likes suffering, but Paul was ready. He even desired to suffer for Christ because suffering brings us closer. My granddad said, as he and my grandbobbie were nearing the end of their lives, that it was the enduring through hard times that made their love more sweet and greater as they aged. In society, we often avoid hardships; we want life to be easy and smooth sailing. But it is often through the hardships and suffering that we become more like Christ—we grow and mature through the suffering when Christ is our focus. Jesus said, "They persecuted Me, they will also persecute you" (John 15:20). When we find our identity in Christ and place our trust and hope in Him, the devil hates it; the world hates it, and they will try to persuade us to turn away from Christ, to find our identity in something or someone else. They will persecute us because they do not accept Jesus as Lord. Are we at that level of a relationship with Christ where we are willing to be persecuted for Him? Are we ready to be known as His even though it will mean persecution and suffering?

Being in a family comes with many pros and cons. One of the cons is that when one of my family members is despised by someone, I am hated, too, even if I did nothing. This happened at school when a guy broke up with my sister. All of our friends left me, and I was not even the girlfriend. That is minimal persecution compared to what Christ's followers go through. Nevertheless, I did not mind the loss because I love my sister, and she was safe from a controlling relationship. Our identity cannot be in our friends, or we will not be able to endure. It must be in Christ alone. Paul knows that Christ is worth losing all: relationships, material things, position, wealth, and his very life. How much are we willing to give up to have a life with Christ? This life with Christ here will not be without its sacrifices, but it will be worth it to live with Him in eternity. We need to ask God for His help to be at a place where we count it all as loss for the sake of knowing Him.

Application: Pray as John the Baptist did, that He increases in your life and you decrease. Ask for a great love for Him so that nothing else compares.

How has suffering in your own life shaped your identity?

What are you willing to give up to be identified with Christ? Be specific.

Is there someone in your life who suffers well? What can you learn from their example?

Day Twenty-Nine

Running to Obtain

Philippians 3:12–13

Not that I have already attained, or am already perfected; but I press on, that I may lay hold of that for which Christ Jesus has also laid hold of me. Brethren, I do not count myself to have apprehended; but one thing I do, forgetting those things which are behind and reaching forward to those things which are ahead.

My siblings and I like to do an annual 5K race. While I like the idea of running, I am not a runner, so somewhere at about the one-mile mark I am ready to be done, but that is when my running partner begins to remind me of why I love 5Ks. It is not for the exercise but for the end when I am finished and get to cheer on other runners as they cross the finish line, those who have run the same race I did. I cheer enthusiastically for them because I have run the race and experienced similar challenges. I cheer for complete strangers—I love that part. I want the comradery, the unity of running together with them, because it significantly means more to encourage someone when we have sweat in, panted in, and run in the same race. Here, Paul is referring to the race of Christianity toward God and holiness.

If Paul does not count himself as having obtained, how can I? Paul's mindset is that he can always be growing to be more like Christ. His identity is not found in human perfection but in Christ. Will we ever attain holiness? Possibly. It is attainable, because Jesus set it as a goal for us when He said, "Be holy, for I am holy" (1 Peter 1:16). He would not ask us to do something He has not made possible. Scripture says, "With God all things are possible" (Matthew 19:26). So we press on. Paul is not comfortable with where he is with Christ; he wants to go further and pursue a deeper relationship with Christ; he wants to strive to have the mind of Christ always. His life and religion are not inactive. He is chasing after Christ, running because he wants to catch something. Paul says Jesus has him, now he wants to make sure he has Christ. Christ died for us and has us in His heart; do we have Him in ours? "Press on" is an action. Is our faith with Christ active? People know when a volcano is active; can they tell with our relationship with Christ? I don't mean are we busy in church things; I mean is our relationship with God thriving, or has it become like the fig tree that had leaves but no fruit (Mark 11:12–25)? That fig tree gave the promise of fruit without giving the life of fruit. Therefore, because it lied, Jesus cursed it. I don't want my life to lie about my relationship with Christ. So what am I? Hot or cold, active or dead, fruitful or cursed?

In verse 13, Paul reveals that he forgets things behind him and reaches forward. Paul is casting off every restraint that would hinder him from doing the will of God. He chooses to keep his focus on things above. His identity is not in the race but in who he runs for. How often do we allow the small things of this world to take our eyes off of Jesus and the purpose He has designed for us? Peter was in the middle of walking on water with Jesus when he allowed the waves to distract him and to turn his head (Matthew 14:30). When we let the waves of life distract us, we begin to sink, like Peter. In my own life I have taken my eyes off of Christ due to some temptation or desire that I start chasing more than Christ. When God removes these focuses, then I begin holding on to Christ again. When a global pandemic hit, it became a time when the whole nation had to keep focused on

God because we got easily distracted with the cares and fears of this world. This really caused me to take my identity in Christ to the next level. Our world was shaken, and we had to ask ourselves if we stood with Christ no matter what. Everything good or bad on this earth will only last for a moment, which is why we forsake all others, press on, and cleave only to Christ. What He has is eternal. We need to get our eyes off the past and the temporary and fix our eyes on things above.

Application: Read 2 Peter 1:5–11. Ask God where you are on Peter's list and begin working from there. If you practice these, Peter says you will not be barren nor unfruitful. May you never be complacent with your faith and relationship with Christ. Ask God to help you press on toward His goal.

How do Paul's words help us understand the journey of finding our identity better?

What are you? Hot or cold, active or dead, fruitful or cursed?

Are you willing to press on, to stand with Christ no matter what?

Day Thirty

Keep Learning

Philippians 3:14

I press toward the goal for the prize of the upward call of God in Christ Jesus.

This morning I thought, *Thank you, Lord, for a new day and Your mercies.* A new day means God's grace and mercy is still upon us. Each day, we can try to do better; each day is another chance to glorify God. Paul, whom we would consider an expert, one who hit the mark perfectly, considered himself not to have obtained the level of relationship with Christ that he desired. So he is always pressing forward toward God's still small voice calling him. It is like any other relationship; you are always learning about the other person. After thirty-four years of marriage, Dad learned that my mom did gymnastics in college. He knows Mom on a level no one else does, and it was a lesson for us that there is always something to learn about your spouse.

Consider how infinitely more there will always be something to learn with the Creator of the universe. Forever will not be long enough to learn all there is to know about God. When we quit learning because we think we know it all, that is when problems arise. We must not think our identity in Christ has reached perfection simply because we have a relationship with Him. Our relationship with Christ is the beginning; we are always to grow more in Him. Stay humble and keep seeking. Those who hunger and thirst after God will be filled (Matthew 5:6). As long as we are living, God has a plan and a purpose for us (Jeremiah 29:11). Therefore, we press on each day to grow closer to God and fulfill His call on our lives, strengthening our identity in Him.

James tells us that those who endure and are found faithful will be given a crown of life (James 1:12). This is the prize Paul is talking about and running to obtain. He does not assume that he has obtained it but strives to endure and reach it. What humility. We must press on and not give up. Forgetting what is behind and pressing on to what is ahead, "many are called, but few are chosen" (Matthew 22:14). The difference between *called* and *chosen* is simply receiving the call and doing something with the call. The chosen ones are those who respond to the call and run the race set before them with endurance (Hebrews 12:1). Life is not a sprint; it is a marathon. So when we feel like we cannot go on, remember, Christ is our rock; when we are weak, He is strong (2 Corinthians 12:10).

I experienced His faithful strength through a baby's death a few years ago. My nephew was born alive, despite the doctor's predictions, and was quickly placed in the neonatal intensive care unit for two weeks. It was not expected that he would live past fourteen days. Through God's mercy, he did live and got to come home so his siblings, aunts, uncles, and grandparents could meet him. Due to the NICU rules, we were unable to see him in the hospital, and only one parent was allowed to briefly see him at a time. He lived forty-nine days, against the odds, and we were blessed to have him as a part of our lives for that long. Every day was a miracle. Don't tell me that my God does not do miracles anymore! Those forty-nine days, you can imagine, were not easy. Tube feeding a newborn was another hardship that came with this journey. Each day was filled with the anxiety of future sorrow but was also in itself a miracle. With everything going on, I would often cry myself to sleep, but every morning God was waiting with a daily dose of strength in Him. The verse that says there may be pain in the night, but joy comes in the morning was very real to me (Psalm 30:5). Never once was His strength not offered. There were days when I did not take it, and there were days when it was just enough strength to get me through the day. By the night it was gone, but He was faithful to offer His help again and again every time I woke up. It was my choice if I took it or not. So turn your eyes to Jesus, for He surely cares for you (1 Peter 5:7).

Application: Lord, help us to always be striving for a better relationship and understanding of You. Give us hearts that yearn for You.

How does God's mercy impact our identity?

What is one way you can keep learning about God?

What would you like to learn about Him next?

How can we keep pressing forward to the goal and call of Christ?

Week Five Overview

What did God teach you about your identity this week?

How do you keep a circumcised heart?

What is the cost of following Jesus?

How can we keep running the race of endurance?

Day Thirty-One

The Mind of Christ

Philippians 3:16

Nevertheless, to the degree that we have already attained, let us walk by the same rule, let us be of the same mind.

The same mind? Which mind is that? It is not my mind, your mind, his mind, or her mind, but it is the mind of Christ. This was a discussion in a Bible study when we read through the book of Philippians. A friend and I were both making a point. I did not want to surrender my mindset for the mindset of one of the guys in the Bible study, and he did not want to surrender to mine. If I surrendered, he was the winner. If he surrendered, I was the winner. If we both surrendered, Christ was the winner, which made us both at peace.

A mindset of humility, obedience, and Christ is seen in Philippians 2:5–8, where Paul is describing Jesus coming as a man and His life here on this earth. I believe if each one of us walks in the mind of Christ, we can be united because we will all have one mind—His. Now, there will be times when we are called to walk different paths because Christ has different jobs for each of us to accomplish. My role in life is different from yours, from my siblings, from my parents' because Jesus has something individually designed for each one of us to do. Regardless of our roles, if we walk by the Spirit, we will not fulfill the lusts of the flesh (Galatians 5:16), and Paul is trying to get us to leave the sinful man behind and walk as the new man in Christ. Paul encourages those who are walking with Christ to continue, to not grow weary, to not fall back, but to strive toward the goal set before us that we may obtain Christ (Philippians 3:12).

We keep going; Christ is not someone to give up on. We should always choose to surrender to His mindset. He deserves our consistency and endurance. Finding our identity in Christ comes at a cost; we must give up all else and follow Him (Luke 9:61–62; 14:33). The man who found the great pearl sold everything for it; he had found an amazing treasure. He did not think anything was too great a price for this gift of God (Matthew 13:45–46). Too many times in this generation we don't think a relationship with Christ is worth a great price. In relationships in general, we give up and walk out because we are weary, hurt, betrayed, or scared. Marriages fall apart, churches fall apart, and friendships fall apart, but worst of all our relationship with Christ falls apart if we are not careful, if we choose not to endure hardships and things we do not understand. We have become lazy in our relationships.

Running takes work. As mentioned before, my siblings and I enjoy doing 5K races twice a year, and I am not a good runner. I have to train my body to endure a 3.1-mile run. If I want to be able to run the whole thing, it takes months of work and practice for me. Reality is that if we want to be good at anything, it takes work, especially relationships.

The relationships with Christ and our families (spouse, siblings, and children) are worth the work because God calls us and expects us to work at these. His heart is broken when we fall away from Christ. I believe it also makes Him heartbroken when families fall apart. He hates divorce. God gave us a spouse, siblings, and our children, and He expects us to trust Him and work with what He gave us.

In everything, we are to keep striving through the challenges and hardships of life to be more like Christ. We cannot let the challenges of life stop us from a pursuit of Christ. We are to honor God, as Christ did, when things get hard and trust Him to help us stick it out. We must not become lazy in our walk with Christ. In hardships and challenges, we seek to know His mind because He is the only One with the answers of how to navigate through them in a manner that honors the Father.

Application: Lord, give us dedication to stick with You through thick and thin. Please teach us and help us to surrender our minds to the mind of Your Son, Jesus Christ. Help us grow in our relationship with Christ.

How does having the mind of Christ affect your identity?

Which mind are you keeping? Yours or Christ's? How can we work on keeping His mindset?

What does it mean to you to have the mind of Christ?

Day Thirty-Two

Be an Example to Follow

Philippians 3:17

Brethren, join in following my example, and note those who so walk [with the mind of Christ], as you have us for a pattern.

As a middle child, I had the opportunity to both learn from the examples of my older siblings and be an example to my younger ones. For example, as I watched the older ones start Bible studies on campus or be generous, I made note and wanted to follow in their footsteps. I distinctly remember that one of them, whenever we went out with her, tried hard to make it a special day, so when I had my own job, I tried to make a trip to the store or an outing something fun for my younger siblings too. As to being an example to the younger ones, this could mean I was a good example or a bad one. How I responded to corrections from my parents would influence how they treated our parents, because if Moriah could get away with it, they could too. Or when I could hear myself coming out of a younger sibling's mouth. There are some places in which I see I was a bad example, not keeping my side of the room clean or talking back to authorities; neither of these taught my younger siblings to honor their parents. When you know someone is watching and learning from you, the failure feels even more weighty. The pressure is on to do well. Sometimes just realizing the impact of that keeps me striving for holiness. We all have those who watch us. Will you set an example of someone who lives for Christ with all that they are?

Christ did not leave us to walk this path alone; He sent His Holy Spirit and gave us examples in those who have walked before us. Being raised in a family of ten children provided my siblings and me many examples and gave many as well. I am number six, so I had the privilege to learn from the mistakes of my older siblings or try to reach the bar set by them that seemed impossibly high. I also was given instructions of what was expected from a big sister. It went something like this: "You are the big sister. You have to set a good example for your younger siblings. They look up to you, and to whom much is given, much is expected." When I succeeded, I helped set the standard for good behavior, obedience, and trusting God, and when I failed, it was an example of what not to do. Those older siblings helped set the standard. They showed me that it was possible to reach the biblical ideas and standards set by our parents.

One goal I set for myself, which was simply physical, was to pass the driver's test on the first try. Everyone before me had done so. Another of my goals was to pass biology class with an A in lab and lecture, because one sibling got a B in both and the other got only a B in lab. I set my goal. I wanted to do better. A goal I did not set for myself was to be single. Some of my sisters were single until they were in their thirties. This was not my idea of a goal for me, but as each year passed and I got older, their waiting on God became a mile marker to me. Their examples let me know it was possible to be content, single in Christ, in our thirties, still be beautiful, still serve God, and not fall off the deep end. I have indeed joined the ranks of these sisters now (although some have since gotten married), but their examples are still ones I look at to keep my focus on God and the identity He has given me to walk in right now. My sisters had to teach themselves to not have their identity etched in the imaginings of the future, nor the losses of the past, but to sink their roots deeply into their identity in Christ. They bravely fought, trusting Him for who He destined them to be, trusting that their stories would be an example that brings glory to God and encourages others along the way. These are godly examples to look for and to imitate. They give a tangible example and a strength to others walking on the same path.

We will overcome by the blood of the Lamb and the word of the testimony (Revelation 12:11). Do you have Bible heroes? Are there people you know who show you how to overcome through their identity being found in Christ? Testimonies of God's people following Him give us hope, peace, and endurance. They are role models, just like my older siblings, who fashion their lives after Christ as they follow Him. Dad says, "Every Paul needs a Timothy, and every Timothy needs a Paul." Have a testimony that is never too proud to learn from others and never too busy to teach others when asked. Dad used to say, "Where I mess up, don't do it. Learn from my mistakes and don't repeat them. Where I do well, I hope you exceed me and do even better." No one will be perfect, but follow them as they follow Christ (1 Corinthians 11:1). *As they follow Christ* is the key phrase. When we see a good pattern of Christian living, we need to emulate it. However, do not be like Ananias and Sapphira, who saw Barnabas get recognized for his generous gift-giving. They sold land and lied about the proceeds in order to gain status and favor as Barnabas did (Acts 5:1–11). They were too caught up in an identity of being in the recognition and praises of people. A mindset like Christ's is not about the recognition and status of people; it is about glorifying our Father in heaven and encouraging other believers in the ways of Christ. We want to be around people who have the same mindset—Christ's. They will help us stay focused on Him.

There are times and seasons in everyone's life; a time to teach and a time to be taught. Always, though, be an example. God often puts people in our lives for a time who will help grow us closer to Him. Maybe a person is unknowingly teaching us self-control and patience because they are grating us the wrong way. How wonderful if it may be someone who is teaching us the ways of God and we are just paying attention and absorbing it. Maybe God has sent you an encourager. There will also be others who are Christ-centered, but they may be young in their faith. These are the ones we teach if they will allow themselves to be taught by us. My little brother was one who encouraged me. At age fifteen he began absorbing and implementing the mind of Christ in ways that all I could do was watch in amazement of what God was doing in his life. To watch him have godly fruit of the Spirit and grow in God was exhilarating. Whichever situation, remember it is only for a season, so learn and grow as much as you can in what Christ is teaching you. We all can follow good examples of believers and be an example for others to learn from. As we walk in Christ's footsteps and think His thoughts, we can show others the way to Christ's mind too.

Application: Ask God to help you grow in Him, to learn what He is teaching, and to be aware of the season. Ask for a Paul to teach you and a Timothy for you to teach.

How is being an example a key aspect of finding your identity?

What are some wrong areas in which we can get our identity caught?

How can you be an example to others in helping them find their identity in Christ?

Day Thirty-Three

Transformed

Philippians 3:21

Who will transform our lowly body that it may be conformed to His glorious body, according to the working by which He is able even to subdue all things to Himself.

One year, my two older sisters and I went with a friend to the Smoky Mountains in Tennessee. We saw many wooden bear carvings. We watched a man pull out a three-foot-long hunk of wood and begin to take a chainsaw to it. He worked for hours, but with his precision, he transformed this stump into a little bear standing on its back feet with a fish in its front paws. Wow! The time and precision that went into transforming the wood was amazing. He saw a log and knew what it would become and what needed to happen to get it there. Even my crocheting teacher, my neighbor who is more like family, tells me that you see the yarn and know what it is going to be made into. Personally, this has only happened a few times with me, and once it was with a hat. I saw the yarn and instantly thought "you will be a hat, and I will give you away to someone specific." God does the same with us. He sees who we are meant to be and puts us through chainsaws and crochet hooks to form and fashion our identity into what it is meant to be. But only through His hands and work will we get to the end result.

Check yourself. Are you being transformed to the ways of God or are you being conformed to the things of this world?

What or who is designing your identity? Do you allow God to chip away at your sin and make you a glorious creation? Our chainsaw-carving Master Craftsman will often start with a thick block of wood and cut and chip away the excess things that do not add to His end design. If God, our master craftsman, does not cut and chisel away on our lives, we will simply be useless blocks, or if He begins and we do not allow Him to finish, then we are a mangled up, distorted, unidentifiable creation.

We are Christians, "like Christ," "little Christs" that are to shine the way to the One True Christ and Savior. If we are to look like Him there are a lot of things that need to be removed. But we like to hold on to things because we think they are ours. We think our bark and rough exterior and experiences define who we are, but they don't. Only the Master Carpenter defines who we are. All things created belong to God—even us. He gives and He takes away, and we are to bless His name for it (Job 1:21). Everything we have—our homes, our jobs, our families, even our bodies—is on loan to us. God wants us to learn to say "blessed be the name of the LORD," as Job did when everything was taken from him. One day it will come time for God to take it all away, because it will no longer be needed to make the image of Christ in our lives. Our time here will be up, and we will understand that nothing is ours, so we must let it go. Remember the old Serenity Prayer? It is a prayer that asks God to help us keep everything in perspective and to trust Him with what we do not have control over. If we don't give everything to God, we are like children holding on to something they have no control over. This prevents us from being the masterpiece God desires us to be.

What are you holding on to that is not yours? You think it is, so you will not relinquish it to the One who gave it. If that stump held on to its roots, its bark, its branches, it would have never transformed into that masterpiece of a cute bear holding his little fish, and it would have no value. Why is it so hard to let go of our own identity? Because we don't trust the One who is calling us to give it to Him. Because we can't see the full picture, and we think what we have is best. At least that is my struggle in letting go. If you are like me, you ultimately do not trust that He will do what is best for you. Every time something comes up, I have to choose to surrender it to God. God says He will do what is best (Jeremiah 29:11). Do we choose to believe Him? Will we choose to trust God today? He has never forsaken the righteous (Psalm 37:5). He has never lied; He cannot. He is always faithful. He has never failed us and never will! Will you choose to trust Him and allow Him to transform your identity into the woman and design of life He sees in you?

Application: Pray and ask God to give you the strength to let go. Ask Him to continue to chip away the excess so you might be His perfect masterpiece.

How is surrendering to the design of Christ forming your identity in Him?

What do you have in your life that needs to be chipped away?

Why is it so hard to let go?

Can God be trusted with your heart?

How will you trust God with the parts of your life He has asked for?

Day Thirty-Four

Reboot with Praise

Philippians 4:4

Rejoice in the Lord always. Again I will say, rejoice!

Every child typically is taught by their parents and society to say thank you, even if we receive something we do not like. But when we receive a disappointing gift, how can we be thankful? Look beyond the gift; it is important to be appreciative of the heart behind the giver. Sometimes in life we are given things by God that do not seem to be what we wanted. Nevertheless, we are to act as Christ did; we are to trust the One who gave it and thank Him for it anyway. One year I found myself complaining a lot about life in general. To help curb this destructive habit, God had me begin a gratitude list. If I write down only three things I am grateful for each day, by the end of a year, I will have more than one thousand precious things I am grateful for. This is beneficial both for my mind and spirit. It helps me look for the good in every day.

No matter our circumstances, nothing changes the fact that God is good. Therefore, we always have a reason to rejoice in the Lord. Giving thanks and praise is extremely important because it reboots our mindset and fights the attitude our enemy wants us to have. When my older sister is very down or frustrated at the events of life, she begins making a list of all the things she is thankful for concerning her circumstances, or she plays the piano and sings to God to fight the temptations of the enemy to succumb to anger or depression. Praise drowns out the complaining accusations of the enemy. I know I need to practice this more to have the mind of Christ. When we give thanks, we are reminded of the goodness of God, and it drowns out the lies of the enemy. As our minds realign and we recount what God has done, we find peace because God gives us His peace. We know He will answer all these concerns of our hearts that we are choosing to praise Him in. Scripture encourages us that in prayer, supplication, and thanksgiving, let your request be made known to God (Philippians 4:6).

We must remember to find joy in our circumstances, even in times of persecution and disappointment. The book of Matthew says, "Blessed are those who mourn, / For they shall be comforted. . . . Blessed are those who are persecuted for righteousness' sake, / For theirs is the kingdom of heaven" (Matthew 5:4, 10). Job praised God when everything, save his wife, was taken away from him; he said, "The LORD gave, and the LORD has taken away; / Blessed be the name of the LORD" (Job 1:21). We can rejoice always because our salvation is in Him and not in the perishable things of this life that have us worrying or downhearted. Paul, of all people, had something to mourn and groan about because he was in prison, yet he says to rejoice. If he can rejoice in prison, we can rejoice in life. Our identity does not come from our circumstances but from Christ alone. Be grateful for the little things. When we become complainers and ungrateful people, that is when our mindsets begin to shift. We must be careful not to allow our mindsets to become accusatory toward God and what He is doing. His plans are always best for us despite how we feel. And it is often in those hard times when we praise Him that we grow closer to Him, and our identity in Him becomes more confident. Trust Him and rejoice because our good heavenly Father watches over us, and He cares for us (Matthew 6:30).

Application: Pray and give yourself reminders to practice thankfulness and praise.

How does praise impact your identity?

What are three things you are grateful for today?

What is a way you can choose to praise instead of complain?

Day Thirty-Five

Prayer

Philippians 4:6–7

Be anxious for nothing, but in everything by prayer and supplication, with thanksgiving, let your requests be made known to God; and the peace of God, which surpasses all understanding, will guard your hearts and minds through Christ Jesus.

When we pray, it gives us a moment to pause and allow God to put things into perspective, if we will be still before Him. Our nation always needs prayer, but one particular year my heart was in anguish for my country. As my heart would fret, I spoke about my anguish to the group of young adults I was meeting with for Bible study. In talking together, to my surprise, I realized that my identity was too tightly wrapped up in being an American in the land of the free, the home of the brave. Thankfully that burden for my nation pushed me to trust more in my God, not in my country or the government but in God alone. The suggestion of one of the guys at Bible study became our challenge: Be the Daniels of our time and pray on behalf of our nation. As we began to pray, the problems did not go away, but our hearts would rest more in Christ. Despite the turmoil, He was ultimately in control and that meant it would be OK. Every week, we would close Bible study with all of us praying for our country. God impressed it upon me to take it further. Everyday on my lunch break I would get on my knees in my car (it was cramped) and intercede for my homeland. This refocus on my identity in Christ truly released some of my anxiety about my nation. Once we have things in the right perspective and order, we are able to work more efficiently for God and others. God wants to hear what is going on in our hearts. As He listened to me and gave counsel, my anxious heart found peace and a balance that anchored me. As we trust Him and stop being anxious about our world and ourselves, we remind our hearts to have joy and to trust God. This is a process of prayer.

The same year I was learning to trust God with my country, several friendships abruptly ended, and surprisingly I was giving thanks. I knew in my soul that thanksgiving was the pathway to release and to trusting God. It took many days and, for some, months until I was broken and humble enough to honestly and actually be thankful for the pain of losing my friends. But I had to experience what David said, "Why are you downcast, O my soul? . . . / Hope in God" (Psalm 43:5).

We Christians know where hope, joy, and peace come from; so why do we spend so little time in prayer? Our most powerful position is on our knees, when we bow and submit to the Father. James tells us, "Submit to God. Resist the devil and he will flee from you. Draw near to God and He will draw near to you" (James 4:7–8). When we truly pray and seek the mind of Christ above our agenda, our needs, our wants, and even our own identity, we will submit to God and resist the devil. As we take time away from our loud, demanding world and come to God in prayer, He speaks "Peace, be still," over our chaotic lives. He says, "Be still, and know that I am God" (Psalm 46:10). Between my identity as an American and through my friendships, I had to still myself that whole year. Prayer can calm us when we pause our noise, activities, and lists long enough to listen for the "still small voice" of God (1 Kings 19:11–13). When we listen, God speaks; when we obey, God moves; and when God moves, things happen. How often are we quiet and still in the presence of God? As a child, I did not enjoy holding still, and that still plays into my prayer life. I still don't like holding still, but I make myself because when I am still is when I gain the mind of Christ and am redirected in accordance with His will. When was the last time we quieted ourselves and basked in the presence of our Father, Almighty God?

Application: Lord, help us draw near to You to be calmed and filled. Lord, please come and dwell in us; fill us with Your peace that passes all understanding (Philippians 4:7).

How does prayer shape your identity?

What are you anxious about right now? How does that affect your identity in Christ?

What are you praying about?

What do you need to give over to God?

Day Thirty-Six

My Thoughts

Philippians 4:8

Finally, brethren, whatever things are true, whatever things are noble, whatever things are just, whatever things are pure, whatever things are lovely, whatever things are of good report, if there is any virtue and if there is anything praiseworthy—meditate on these things.

When I was in elementary school, this verse was the Wednesday night memory verse for the girls' program. This truth was established in me decades ago, but like most things, it did not automatically become my mindset. Somedays I still struggle with it. The truth instilled took a long time to grow fruitful—until I was in my twenties. At that time, God showed me that this verse was a measuring stick with which to analyze my thoughts. If my thoughts did not line up with this list, then they most likely needed to be taken captive and disposed of. So I had a list of questions I would ask myself about the thought. The first question I would ask myself was, Is it true? If it passed *true*, then I asked, Is it noble? Few thoughts got past the first two questions, but if they did, I would keep going down the list. This exercise still helps keep my mind and my identity clean before God and people.

Part of keeping our mind on Christ is thinking about the right things. Paul tells us in 2 Corinthians to take every thought captive to the obedience of Christ (2 Corinthians 10:5). Once we take our thoughts captive and give them to Christ, we have an empty space. Now we must fill our minds with right thoughts. If we don't, the Bible gives us the illustration of a house. If there are demons in a house and they have been rebuked and cast out, then our house is clean. However, if we do not fill our home with God, it is simply an empty home, and the demons will come back seven times worse (Matthew 12:43–45). Our soul is like our spiritual home. It is the deepest part of us. One of the doors into our home, like a channel into our soul, is through our mind. Therefore, we must keep our mind set on Christ and the things of God so that we can protect our home, our soul.

Paul gave us a list and a standard to think about. He basically said these are the types of thoughts we should dwell on, anything else needs to be gotten rid of. Now if a thought does not meet the standards listed in the verse, we must use that as a warning sign to take the thought captive and not let it into our souls. A thought goes into our souls when we dwell and meditate on it. It only becomes a part of our identity if we let it. We can control who we become by what we allow ourselves to think about. Before we accept an idea, it is just a thought. So when we meditate on thoughts that have the characteristics of this list of virtues, we are putting goodness, health, and life into our souls. However, when we focus on ungodly thoughts and temptations, we put poison in our souls. We may not realize it at first. They may seem good, like sugar, but the overall effect is unhealthy and nonnutritious to our spiritual well-being. Like unhealthy foods, evil thoughts add unnecessary weight that holds us back from our best. It may be a tempting poison that feels good, but chocolate-covered poison is still poison. It will damage our souls and slowly kill us if we keep eating it.

Take your thoughts captive and think on the virtuous things in Philippians 4:8. Let's use this as a measuring stick. Work your way down the list. Does the thought align with the mindset of

Christ? Our primary questions should be: Is this thought true? Is this thought noble? Is this thought just? Is this thought pure? Is this thought lovely? Is this thought of good report? Is this thought virtuous or praiseworthy? If only we practiced this every time, we would be better Christians and possibly be further along in having the mind of Christ.

Application: We praise You, O Lord, for these warning signs and ask for Your endurance to continually take thoughts captive to Your obedience when they don't match up with Your list.

How do your thoughts contribute to your identity?

Your thoughts shape your identity. How can you take your thoughts captive to the obedience of Christ?

What is the first thing to ask yourself about a thought?

What is something true about your identity in Christ?

How is your thought life?

Week Six Overview

What did God teach you about your identity this week?

How do praise and thanksgiving shape your identity in Christ?

How can you be an example to others in having your identity in Christ?

What does God want you to think on, and how can you direct your thoughts to achieve that?

Day Thirty-Seven

Contentment

Philippians 4:11

Not that I speak in regard to need, for I have learned in whatever state I am, to be content.

Contentment is a beautiful and valuable asset that we often overlook. It is a foundation that is ready for God to build upon. When we were little, we did not have much, but if you had asked any one of us, we would never have believed we were poor. We did not travel to amazing sites, we did not have elaborate Christmases, and we did not all have our own rooms. Instead of visiting monumental sites, our backyard was filled with stick forts and makeshift teepees where historic imaginary battles were fought and won. For Christmas, we baked goodies for neighbors, made gifts for one another, and all sat around while Dad read the Christmas story from the Gospels of Matthew and Luke. Instead of each of us having our own room, there was always someone to talk to, to sing to you if you were frightened, or to tell stories to help you fall asleep. It may not have been contentment on my part because I did not know any different, but it was on the part of my parents. They chose to be content with the little we had and taught us to thrive in it. The contentment they exemplified and taught was a foundation that would set the course for our lives as adult men and women. I cannot imagine a better childhood.

We can best serve God when we are content with where He has us. He has asked us to wait on Him, to glorify Him in the season we are in. Who are we to complain about where He has us? Wouldn't that be like clay telling the potter that it doesn't want to be a pot (Isaiah 45:9)? God has a plan for each one of us; it is our job to ask God what it is and to strive to fulfill His plan. He knows the identity He has etched within each of us, and His plans will draw it out, refine it, and complete it. I have often thought that even if I could tell my younger self God's plans for me and what He would do, I probably would not have believed me. I was a young girl who hated reading and expected to get married around the same age her mother did. As a grown woman, who is still single, who has written books for the Lord, and who has planned young adult conferences for many years, I don't know that I would have thought this was God's plan. Nevertheless, as always, His plans have a special beauty to them when we walk in His service. God's plans are best. His plans are not ours, but they are always perfect. We may not understand them, for His ways are higher than ours (Isaiah 55:9), but His ways are good. Contentment is not about understanding; it is about trusting God. Did I have tears when I reached that age and was not married yet? Yes, but marriage is not my identity; my identity is found in Christ. Marriage may be part of His plan or it may not. We just have to trust Him. When I look back, I see His faithfulness and the wholesome goodness of His plans. From a little girl who fought tanks in her imagination to a woman who is called to surrender dreams daily and fight her imaginations to keep the mind of Christ, our Lord has an acute way of conforming us to the image of Christ.

We should be grateful and content for the opportunity to serve, no matter how humble. Jesus, the God of the universe, came down as a helpless child who could do nothing for Himself. He honored His parents when they corrected Him for being in the temple as a young boy because He conceded to the reproof, willingly went with them, and submitted to the authority of His earthly parents (Luke 2:41–52). Scripture does not record Jesus ever doing this again as an adolescent, therefore we conclude that He adhered to the wisdom of his parents and honored their decision. As an adult, He allowed Himself to be beaten, spat upon, and ultimately killed by weak humans who had no authority over their God (Mark 15:16–20). What humility to come and be under the authority of humans. We, too, ought to humble ourselves before God. Accept the lowly jobs; those who can be trusted with little will be given much (Luke 16:10).

For those of us who are in a change between seasons, we are to be thankful for the past season and ready to move and grow in another season. As I once contemplated a season change in my life, I was afraid and sad. This happened during a change in the natural season. It made me excited and happy to see the leaves change around me and feel the air get brisk. You would have thought it was Christmas. As I walked in this state of joy, the Lord said to me, "You are so excited about season changes in the weather; why are you not excited about the changes in your life?" Physical season changes bring the promise of something long awaited. Spiritual season changes bring the promise that God will be faithful again. We may have gotten comfortable with where He has us, but comfortable and content are very different. Comfortable is in the situation, and we don't want to move. Content is in Christ, and we are willing to let go of the current season and move forward to the next because we trust that He is good and knows what is best for us (Romans 8:27–37).

Application: Pray and ask God to teach you to be content in the season He has you. Ask Him for the ability to serve Him in this season.

How does contentment play a role in finding your identity in Christ?

What season change are you facing right now?

How can you trust God in the season changes He brings?

Where is God asking you to be content?

Day Thirty-Eight

In His Strength

Philippians 4:13

I can do all things through Christ who strengthens me.

This is true. Like Daniel and David, I have found that whenever God calls us to do something, He will always provide the strength to obey. We may be wiped out at the end of the day, but we will be victorious if we walk wherever Christ leads. A few years back brought one of my biggest tests of obedience. I met a guy volunteering with the community, and a relationship developed. My hope began to spread wings that all my dreams of marriage could finally come true, and then God asked me to say goodbye to this dream. I really thought marriage would help complete my identity. But what I did not realize is that nothing can complete my identity except the One who designed it: God. If I never get married, I am still a child of God. If I do get married, I am first and foremost a child of God. I am called to obey even when it does not make sense and even when it is hard because I am a child of God who is trusting her heavenly Father.

Do not think it cruel that God would ask this of me, it was a test and an opportunity for Him to show me the lengths and depths of His strength in my obedience. Was it painful? Absolutely. Was it worth it? Yes. But God is always good, and in His goodness, He showed me that with Him I can break my own heart for His call because my identity is in Him alone. The rest is just bells and whistles or icing on the cake. Was I exhausted afterward? Yes, but I cannot describe the strength and resolve in the midst of the trial that God gave me to do His will. Am I better for it? Absolutely, because I now know the depths I can go with God. He taught me how far I can go in my obedience. He taught me that He is always there every step of the way with the strength I need.

Paul, who was stoned, shipwrecked three times, and beaten within inches of his life five times, knows that God will strengthen us to accomplish what He has told us to do. God says His word will not return void (Isaiah 55:11). The same power that filled Paul and that dwells in Christ—the Holy Spirit—now dwells in us (Romans 8:11). Therefore, we can face heartbreaks, deaths, tests, trials, changes in seasons, circumstances, and situations. God increases the depths of our identity, who we think we are, with confidence in the One who will see us through and who will give us strength. He will give us everything we need to overcome challenges victoriously. Because of God's Spirit in us, we can face anything and respond appropriately in accordance with His will. His mindset gives us power and perspective. It is a hard battle to keep, but it is true.

Have you ever noticed that when our mind is engaged, we respond to things faster? However, if our mind is disengaged or wandering, it can seem sluggish. The mind of Christ gets us into that humility and submission to the will of the Father, which creates a mind willing to engage. Our minds become involved and in tune to the will of God. Remember our example in Philippians 4:8 when Paul gives us his list of things to think on? Paul's list calls us to engage our minds in the spiritual battle at hand over our thoughts. It teaches us which ones to accept and which ones to reject in order to keep our minds focused on Christ. God gives us the physical strength and the mindset to accomplish His purposes. But in order for us to be effective, we must align ourselves properly—submit to God and resist the devil (James 4:7).

Submit and resist. This is truly hard and has been a struggle for me. Over the last few years there have been many trials in my world, and keeping a positive mindset is difficult. The problem is that my mind has not been resting in Christ and taking thoughts captive as it should. Instead, my thoughts have focused on my disappointments in the trials and have not clung to the provisions of God in the trials. God must stay as my focus. Nothing and no one deserves to be elevated to the position of God, not even in our minds, not even our struggles, not even our emotions. We ought to focus on what God has done and will do, like Jesus, who endured the cross for what would come after it (Hebrews 12:1–2). By submitting to God we are putting ourselves in the position to be used by God. "God resists the proud, / But gives grace to the humble" (James 4:6). Perhaps I have been proud in thinking that because of my walk with God I should not have to go through the trials that have come. But God never promised a life without pain. In fact, He promises if we walk this road with Him there will be pain and persecution, but the end is worth it—He is worth it (Matthew 10:22). He gave everything so we could live, can't we give what He asks for so that He may live through us? Christ will make everything all right after this world ends, if not before.

How does our identity play into this? Jesus said to come as a child (Matthew 18:3). Are we willing to trust Him as a child? A little kid will jump into the deep end of a pool if you are calling them to. They will run with all their might, not worrying about the danger. And a little child believes what they are told. My youngest brother thought he could fly at two years old. He would jump off the back of our couch and never touch the floor because one of his siblings would catch him. Children aren't as afraid as adults. My sister and I are riding bikes again, and I have found that the things I did as a kid on a bike aren't as easy as an adult. I have lost that childlike confidence. May that fearless faith of a child grow in us again because we are trusting in our heavenly Father. When we submit our thoughts and ourselves to the Holy One we can do all the things that He instructs us to do through His strength. Paul was humble and submitted himself to God. Jesus, our example of perfection, submitted and humbled Himself to the Father. How much more should we? And will He help us? A broken and contrite spirit, He will not reject (Psalm 51:17).

Application: Pray for mobility that we will bend and move as Christ's hands guide us so that we will be formed into the pot He is designing, one used by God. The most work can be done when the clay is moldable.

How does God strengthen you on your quest to find your identity?

What trial is God asking you to have strength in?

Where are you identifying yourself that is any place other than God?

Day Thirty-Nine

To the Least of These

Philippians 4:16

For even in Thessalonica you sent aid once and again for my necessities.

Driving to band practice, my older sister noticed a beggar by the church. She and two guys from the band went out and met him. He was thirsty. All they did was give him a drink of water, and they prayed for him. She came home elated and stoked! She believes he was an angel in disguise whom God wanted them to help. We are told by Jesus that if we give a cup of cold water to someone in His name, it is as if we gave it to Him (Mark 9:41). And again, He says what you have done to the least of these you have done unto Me (Matthew 25:40).

It is important for the church to be the hands and feet of Christ, especially to a member of the body of Christ, as the Philippians did for Paul. The people of Philippi seemed to have a very generous nature, which we can learn from. The Bible says when we have two items of clothing, let us give one to someone who has none (Luke 3:11). James tells us if we see a brother who asks for food because he is starving and we send him away with prayer but without giving him necessities, we have done no good (James 2:16). If we are able, God expects us to help. When God's people are hungry, or anyone for that matter, feed them. When they have nothing, share what God has given. When we bless people from what we have, we are giving to God. In the book of Matthew, when the "goats" and the "sheep" are being judged, they both ask, "Lord, when were You in prison; when were You hungry and begging bread; when were You naked and needing clothes?" He answers them, "What you have done (or not done) to the least of these you have done to Me" (Matthew 25:40–45). Both the goats and the sheep did not see the others as if they were Jesus in need, but what they did about the need they saw made all the difference between them hearing "Come, you blessed of My Father" and "Depart from Me, you cursed." The goats looked for their identity in their own works; the sheep found their identity in the Good Shepherd. It did not matter what was asked of them; they did it as unto the Lord.

We must use discernment and obedience when we are the hands and feet of Jesus. Obedience is the key. Sometimes God will impress upon us to help. Other times we are told to wait. Our job is to obey. Our identity cannot even be that we give and serve. No, it is to be in Christ alone that we obey no matter if He says to go and do or to be still and wait. Obedience is better than sacrifice (1 Samuel 15:22). Jesus did not heal the lame man at gate Beautiful. Gate Beautiful is by the temple, and we know Jesus passed there often, yet we also know that He did not heal this man because we read of the account when the man is healed by Peter and John in the book of Acts. Why did Jesus not heal this man? Because He obeyed and did only what the Father said and did (John 5:19). The man at gate Beautiful was for Peter and John to heal after Christ's resurrection (Acts 3:2–11). Maybe it was so that the people would see that miracles did not stop just with Jesus's physical presence but that people could be healed in His name. Whatever the case, it brought glory to God for Peter and John—not Jesus—to heal the man. Obey God; when He says, "Move," go; when He says, "Stay," be still. In whatever we do, let us glorify our Father in heaven.

In order to be ready to give, I will challenge you as my sister did me in her devotional for a Bible study we led. She encouraged us to budget our generosity separate from our tithes and offerings. When I have budgeted something, I feel free to spend it within the category allotted. So when God says, "Give," I can give without begrudging and give an amount already determined between God and myself. Listen and obey. Be willing to give to whomever God directs and how He guides. Do not look down on the lowly, and never idolize the famous. We are to serve God where He has placed us and to whom He sends us.

Application: Today pray for obedience and opportunities to be the hands and feet of Jesus so that we may glorify our Father in heaven. Ask yourself, "Will I serve the least of these?"

How is serving the "least of these" essential to building your identity?

Where is one place we can serve others?

How are you doing in obeying God and/or how can you improve it?

Is He telling you to be still or to move?

Why is obedience essential to identifying with Christ?

Day Forty

Fuller than Full

Philippians 4:18

Indeed I have all and abound. I am full, having received from Epaphroditus the things sent from you, a sweet-smelling aroma, an acceptable sacrifice, well pleasing to God.

One year I was contemplating the Beatitudes and the only one I felt I could obtain was the hungering and thirsting for righteousness, so I prayed for it. That one had the promise of being filled. At that time, I knew I was not poor in spirit, mournful, meek, merciful, nor a peacemaker, and I did not want to be persecuted, so I prayed for the only one I thought I was a candidate for. Silly me; God wants us to be full, to receive all of them. His power is not stunted or limited based on us and our ability. He can give us any of the Beatitudes if we only ask. Please let me encourage you not to be stuck in what you think you can do but let God grow you in what He wants for you. Don't limit God or His work in your life. He knows what we need in order to be the person He designed us to be even before any of us were born. Ask and you will receive; seek and you will find (Matthew 7:7).

I want to focus on the concept of being "full." Earlier in Philippians, Paul talked about learning to be content in all things; I believe if I am full with Jesus, I can be content. This concept of being full with Jesus is like our spirits being whole. There is a hole in every human being, and the only one who can fill that void is Jesus Christ.

I asked a friend at a Bible study to share her story of finding her identity in Christ. When she sent me her story, there were two main times in her life when she experienced an emptiness because her identity was rooted in something other than Christ. The first one was when she was nineteen years old. Both her parents died within a few months of each other. Her whole life went through a spiral of pain and loss. Her future plans as a normal teenager collapsed. She was thrust into responsibilities and the need to be self-sufficient overnight. College and dreams were put on hold. But worst of all, she lost meaning and purpose in her life. Feeling like an orphan caused her to become lethargic because there was no one at home to make proud. She had to deal with loneliness and a loss of identity. She was not anyone's daughter anymore, so who was she? Comparison and attempts to fill the hole in her soul were constant struggles. But then Jesus met her in the middle of her identity crisis. Christ led her to the place where her true identity was found. He reminded her that she was never truly alone: "Be strong and of good courage; do not be afraid, nor be dismayed, for the LORD your God is with you wherever you go" (Joshua 1:9). He helped her see that everything happens for a reason, even when she does not understand it. His love is unlike any other—and once she experienced it, it became enough. Over time, as she built her relationship with the Lord, that hole in her heart began to heal. She found peace. She was someone's daughter; she was God's daughter. She trusts in the plans He has for her life even if she does not understand where He is leading. She strives to honor and make Him proud with all that He gives her to do.

The second area where she struggled with her identity being found somewhere other than Christ was in how she looked. For years she struggled to be "enough" in her appearance and presentation to the world. This led her down a destructive path—straight into an eating disorder. It got to the point where she did not recognize herself anymore, and her health, relationships, and even her personality began to disappear. When she tried to be "enough," she lost herself. Her path back to her identity in Christ was not an easy one because the enemy tried to stop her with the lies she had believed before. But God taught her, as a loving Father, what it means to take every thought captive (2 Corinthians 10:5). As she dug into the Word, God showed her who she truly was: "fearfully and wonderfully made" (Psalm 139:14), chosen and called "out of darkness into His marvelous light" (1 Peter 2:9), unshakably loved, no matter what (Romans 8:38–39). In God's eyes, your identity isn't tied to your appearance. While people focus on the outward, the Lord sees the heart (1 Samuel 16:7). As someone who is freely walking in her identity in Christ, my friend wanted to tell you, "God wants to give you a new confidence—rooted in Him. You are so much more than your size, your skin, your style, or your shape. In Christ, you are made new. And in that new identity, you'll find purpose, peace, and a fulfillment that no outward image could ever give you." When she found her identity in Christ, she became whole and full.

Declaring our identity in Christ is not a one and done, it is a constant choice. My friend's life is an example that these struggles are real and reoccurring, but Christ is where we can find enduring peace and fullness. According to scripture, we are to be full and overflowing with Jesus. David says, "[He anoints] my head with oil; my cup runs over" (Psalm 23). A relationship with Christ should be one in which I want to overflow with Him, satisfied with who He made me to be and trusting in Him. In most relationships, we want to know the other person more and more; that is what overflowing is, a consistent outpouring and filling up again. We get filled up by learning about Jesus, and we pour out by sharing Him with others and serving Him. "Blessed are those who hunger and thirst for righteousness, For they shall be filled" (Matthew 5:6).

Jesus wants to fill us up, but so often, we let things of this world tear us down or fill us instead. They stop us from pursuing a deeper relationship with Christ. They block our flow and the passage to our souls. For some of us, getting Jesus was enough. But just getting Him is a possession not a relationship. With a relationship, every day you spend with that person you grow closer together. For some relationships it gets to the point where we want to see them all day every day. Where are we with Christ? Do we just have Him or are we wanting to see Him every day? In my life, when I finally was content in Christ and who I was in Him, I was able and free to do the most work for Him. Thinking back on it, it was when I sought Him most and wanted to learn because I was hungry and thirsty for Him.

Application: Plead with God to fill you with Himself. Ask Him to fill you with His Word, His love, and His wisdom. Now ask to be overflowing with Him so that others may see Him in you.

How can you fill yourself up with Christ to form and fashion your identity in Him?

Where are you finding your identity? Is it in opinions of others, like my friend? Or is it in growing closer to Christ and becoming who He wants you to be?

What truths can anchor your identity in Christ?

Day Forty-One

God Provides

Philippians 4:19

And my God shall supply all your need according to His riches in glory by Christ Jesus.

Fun fact for today: My name, Moriah, means "land where God provided." It is based on the story in which Abraham goes to sacrifice Isaac on Mount Moriah in obedience to the Lord, and God provides a ram in the thicket to be sacrificed instead of Abraham's only son. I distinctly remember one trip my parents had to go on, and we kids were left on our own under the supervision of our adult siblings. Before they left, Mom called me to the car door and said, "Remember your story." She meant the story of Mount Moriah in the Bible, where God tested Abraham and provided another sacrifice instead of the one He asked for. I do not know why God had her tell me that then, but He has used that so many times to guide me and keep my mind stayed on Him, like Abraham's was. Through planning a conference and in my own personal life, I have had to rely on the provision of God multiple times. He has always provided exactly what was needed. I admit it may not be what was wanted, but it was always what was best, and that is the story behind the meaning of my name. When God asks us to do something crazy, it may not make sense, and we may not understand how it works with what else He has told us. Yet we simply obey, and He will provide what is truly needed.

Paul is passing on the hope he has in Christ to the church. We have a good Father in heaven waiting to help us; Jesus tells us, all we have to do is ask (John 14:13). James says, "You do not have because you do not ask. You ask and do not receive, because you ask amiss, that you may spend it on your pleasures" (James 4:2–4). God will supply all our needs—not all our wants, necessarily, but all our needs according to His riches and His glory, not ours. It is not about us. We are to bring glory to God, as Christ did through His life. Paul had learned to be content with nothing. God sent him what he needed so many times through others (Philippians 4:18). Jesus tells us to look at the birds of the air and the flowers of the field and says to us, "I love you more than these, of course I will take care of you" (Matthew 6:28, 31).

So then why are we so anxious? Do we think we have to know the future so it will all work out, or do we want to know so we can decide if we think that is the best option for us? Just let go and trust God. Let Him provide in accordance with His goodness. He knows what we need before we ask Him (Matthew 6:8). The problem is when we think our needs are greater than what His provision will be. That is pride and not trusting in the Lord. That is wanting what we want more than what He has for us, like a spoiled brat. If we find ourselves at that point, we need to humble ourselves, repent, and ask for the mind of Christ to see how His provisions are more than enough for our situation. His thoughts are not our thoughts, and His ways are not our ways; they are higher (Isaiah 55:8–9). They are perfect, and at the end of time, we will be able to look back and see how truly good they were and how blessed we were. He knows the plans He has for us, and they are good, even in bleak circumstances like the children of Israel were in when He spoke those words to them (Jeremiah 29:11). God will supply all our needs. We may actually find we did not need as much as we thought.

Remember to be content. Our heavenly Father is good; His love and mercy endure to all generations (Psalm 100:5). We can trust Him. He did not put us in this world so He could watch us fight and fail. He put us on this earth so that we could live for, learn about, and love Him. Mom has always told us that we are in school here on this earth, and when we graduate, we will go and live with Him forever. Jesus works all things together for good to those who love Him and are called by Him (Romans 8:28). He came to glorify the Father, prepare us, and to save us, which He did for all who will come to Him. When He returned to the Father, He sent the Holy Spirit to teach us how to have a holy mind like Christ, a mind of humble submission and trust. Do you realize that God sent His only Son to die on a cross for us (John 3:16)? Because He did that, we can know that He is love. If that sacrifice is not the love of a good God, I do not know what is. Ask, and He will open up the windows of heaven (Malachi 3:10). James also tells us to ask for wisdom, and God will give it to us without reproach (James 1:5). He is not angry with us when we come before Him again and again asking for the things we need. Our loving Father is willing and waiting for us to just ask Him for good things. If He withholds it, it is for a purpose. And when He gives it, it is to His glory. Life is not about us; it is about Him and who we are in Him. We have nothing to fear. Our God is alive and active in our lives if we will let Him be and keep Him in our thoughts and souls through prayer.

Application: Pray and ask God to give you the peace to be content in the circumstances He has placed you in. Ask Him to show you His provision. Ask also for wisdom and discernment to know when something is a need and to know when to ask for it.

How does trusting God to provide help you allow Him to form your identity?

What are things you want? Now, what are the things you need? Write those out and give them over to God. You can trust Him with them.

Where have you seen the provision of God in your own life?

Day Forty-Two

Glory to God

Philippians 4:20

Now to our God and Father be glory forever and ever. Amen.

Why were you born? This is a question my mom drilled into us children, not in a rude way but to teach us to remember the purpose of every follower of Jesus Christ. She wanted to anchor our minds and our souls to help us know where our identity could always be found. We were put on this earth to serve and bring glory to God through loving Him with all our hearts, minds, and souls and to love our neighbors as ourselves (Matthew 22:37–39). These are the greatest commandments, which give us something to do all the days of our lives in keeping with the mind of Christ.

With Mom's question in mind, we need to ask ourselves, is God glorified in the way we live? Does our lifestyle bring or point others to Jesus? Do we conduct ourselves in a manner that pleases God? We are to do everything to the glory of God (1 Corinthians 10:31) so that when others see us, they see Christ. Let's be real and honest. Someone once said, "Preach the gospel at all times; use words when necessary." Why do we do the things we do? Is it to serve God by loving Him and loving His people? We should not have to tell others; they should know we belong to Jesus by how we live.

When two people start dating, everyone around them can tell. They spend all their time together, hold hands, sit next to each other, laugh at what the other says, finish each other's sentences, and always talk about the other. Can other people tell we are in a relationship with Christ? Can they see His identity fill us? Do we talk about Him as if we spend every day with Him? Is it a more casual relationship or do we spend time with Him and in His word? Are we living to please God, our Love?

This life here is temporary. If you recall the story from day 14 of this book, our life is just a small dash in comparison to life in eternity. Is our dash here on this earth filled with Christ? Did we live it with His eternal mindset? For that to happen, we must spend time with Him. We lose our self-imagined identity to find our true identity in Christ. We want people to look back at our dash of life and say, "Her identity was so steeped in Christ that you met Jesus by just being around her." If God is at the pinnacle of our focus, everything that we do should be done to please Him. Does our mind reflect His? If we walk in His footsteps, we will end up going where He is leading. But in order to do that, we must surrender our idea of our own identity and ask God, allow God, to show us whom He designed us to be.

What brings glory to God? Honoring, worshipping, praising, obeying, giving thanks, talking about what God has done and is doing, loving what He loves, and disliking what He dislikes. Jesus prayed in the garden that God would glorify Him and that He would glorify God (John 17:5). We can glorify God too. In John 21:19, Jesus tells Peter how he will die and glorify God. Even in our deaths God can be glorified. That's a different realization from when I was in college and would pray before every test that I would glorify God on them. I did not know what glorifying meant. In my brain, I was asking to do well so that I brought Him a good name to those around me. That is not a bad prayer. But it was not until I read and comprehended John 21 that I understood glorifying God was so much more. Wanting to glorify God is a good thing, and I still pray that prayer, but I needed the mind of Christ to better understand how to glorify the Father.

I don't have all the answers, but here are some things I've discovered: Perhaps glorifying God is living in such a manner of obedience and submission that others are drawn to Him. Perhaps glorifying God is to profess that His name is above every name, that our lives bow to His will, and that we are willing to die for Him. For each of us, how we live this out may look different. Put aside things that are not of Him and join me in having an identity constantly transformed into the image of Christ through the renewing of our minds, but let all those who claim the name of Jesus Christ be united in one mind—the mind of Christ.

Application: Ask the Lord how you can glorify Him in your life; ask for the mind of Christ and begin to implement what you have learned through this study. As you live out this week, keep two things in mind: Am I glorifying God? And can others see my relationship with Christ? If the answer to either of these two questions is no, what needs to change?

What does it mean to you to glorify God?

How can you glorify God in your identity?

Week Seven Overview

What did God teach you about your identity this week?

Where can you serve others in your life for Christ?

What does it mean to you that God is your provider?

What is the glory of God and how does it impact your identity?

Conclusion

Wow! We have had quite a study. It has challenged me, and I hope it has challenged and encouraged you. Find your identity in Christ by seeking His mind. My last encouragement to you as we wrap this study up is to pray. Pray for strength to have your mind refashioned into the mind of Christ. This is God's will for all His children. It is an endurance marathon not a sprint to have your identity transformed as a child of God. And you can start this race no matter what season of life you are in: young, old, a student, a teacher, a professional in the workforce, a stay-at-home mom, single or married, alone or with a group. He knows these things are part of our lives, but they do not define us. Christ first in our lives will allow us to do the other things well, but we should remember to keep everything in the order that God created first. Gaining the mind of Christ does not happen overnight, but we can begin the process by asking God to help us implement the different aspects of the mind of Christ in our daily thought patterns. In pursuing the mind of Christ, we are to be encouragers and servants. We are to be faithful, loving, unashamed, obedient, humble, content, and merciful. We should have one mind, understand suffering, be unified, endure, pray, capture thoughts, allow God to transform us, remember that He is Lord, and trust God's provision.

May God bless you with the Holy Spirit to whisper to you and remind you of the things He has taught you through this study. May this not be a book that is just put on the shelf after today but one that helps transform you into the image of Christ. When we will lose ourselves and find the mind of Christ, we will find our true, eternal identity. Be blessed, and thank you for walking down this journey with me too.

About the Author

Moriah Hagel is the author of *First and Forever: Singleness in Ephesians* and *Alignment: God's Will or Mine*. She grew up in Wetumpka, Alabama, on a small country ranch. As a young child, Moriah found a great love for God, the Bible, and truth. Moriah has been able to connect these loves and experiences to complex biblical concepts, bringing an understanding of Scripture to her readers. Stories from the ranch, siblings, and Moriah's own personal struggles are shared for the growth of the kingdom of God. "If someone can learn from my struggles, then I intend to share them." Moriah's heart has been to serve God's people, encourage them where they are, and equip them to strive for holiness; she does this through her books and public speaking. This desire also led her to cofound the Seasons Young Adult Conference. Moriah enjoys watching the sun rise, spending time with family, and growing roses.

www.ingramcontent.com/pod-product-compliance
Lightning Source LLC
LaVergne TN
LVHW020059140826
845500LV00028B/250

9781563098024